Psychoanalysis and Faith

THE LETTERS OF SIGMUND FREUD & OSKAR PFISTER

Edited by
HEINRICH MENG *and* ERNST L. FREUD

Translated by
ERIC MOSBACHER

ISBN:978-1-63182-883-6

Printed: March 2023

Published and Distributed By:
Lushena Books
607 Country Club Drive, Unit E
Bensenville, IL 60106
www.lushenabks.com

ISBN:978-1-63182-883-6

CONTENTS

PREFACE

I

THIS volume of correspondence with the Swiss pastor Oskar Pfister is the third collection of Freud's letters to be published. The first consisted of his letters to Wilhelm Fliess from the years 1887 to 1902 and appeared under the title *The Origins of Psycho-Analysis*.[1] The second contained a selection of mainly personal letters to 102 addressees extending over Freud's whole life-time.[2]

We had hoped to publish his correspondence with Pfister in its entirety but, though Freud's original letters have survived, Pfister's have not. Some were destroyed by Freud at Pfister's wish (see letter dated 1.6.1927), and others perished in the hazards of emigration. However, surviving shorthand notes of Pfister's have made it possible to reconstruct his letters and hence to fill in a number of important gaps.

The correspondence began in 1909 and ended in 1937, two years before Freud's death. It consisted altogether of 134 items by Freud, of which nearly a hundred, mostly unabbreviated, are reproduced here.

The editors thank Anna Freud for her help in the work of selection; Professor Herbert Meng's Working Party for Psycho-Hygiene in Basle University, and in particular one of its members Christine M. Senn-Duerck, for their assistance in preparing the material for publication; and Frau Pfister, Pfister's widow, who was assisted by Pastor Pfenninger, for their work on his letters.

Ernst L. Freud .

[1] Imago, London, 1954; Basic Books, New York, 1954
[2] *Letters of Sigmund Freud*. Basic Books, New York, 1960; Hogarth Press, London, 1961

II

OSKAR PFISTER, the youngest of the four sons of a Pr₁
testant pastor, was born in Zürich in 1873. He lost his fath₁
at the age of three. After attending school in Zürich I
studied theology, philosophy and psychology in Züric
Basle and Berlin. His first congregation was at Wald in tl
canton of Zürich, and in 1902 he joined the Zürich circui
of which he remained a member until his retirement in 193
In 1934 he received an honorary degree from the theologic
faculty of the University of Geneva.

His first wife, Erika, *née* Wunderli, died in 1929, leaving
son who is now a psychiatrist in Zürich. His second wife w₁
a widowed cousin, Martha Zuppinger-Urner, who alreac
had two children, to whom Pfister was an admirable fathe

During the first years of his ministry Pfister wrote a pap₁
protesting against 'the sins of omission towards psychology
present-day theology'. In 1908 he came across the work
Freud, which provided him with the tool for which he h₂
long sought, enabling him to give additional aid to tho
whom his spiritual aid alone had been insufficient. He mac
his way to the unconscious and half-conscious sources
anxiety states, doubts of conscience and obsessional ideas
those who sought his help and, in so far as medical interve
tion was not called for, worked with them in loosening up ar
dispersing their psychological difficulties, fixations and r
pressions, and independently laid the foundations of a psych
logically oriented system of education and pastoral work.

Between 1909 and his death in 1956 he published num₁
ous books and papers in which he described his work a₁
observations, in particular on psycho-analytic technique,
the aetiological importance of sexuality in the formation
the neuroses, on religion and hysteria, the psychology of a
philosophy and psycho-analysis, analysis in pastoral wo₁
Christianity and anxiety, and related themes.

A matter of especial concern to him was the application of psycho-analytic findings to education, a field of study to which he gave the name of paedanalysis.

It would be a great mistake to assume that because of his work in the field of psycho-analysis Pfister neglected his pastoral work or his spiritual duties. He was a man incapable of doing things by halves, and in his ministry he was whole-heartedly and utterly sincere, radiating warmth and benevolence and helpfulness to all who turned to him. His friend Pastor Pfenninger writes of him: 'As the representative of a free Christianity he was opposed to all dogma, but he met with understanding and love those who held fast to dogma because of inner ties . . . and he was backed by the love of his congregation.'

His relations with Freud continued through all the years of his ministry and were consolidated in numerous letters and occasional meetings. The two men were real friends. Their correspondence demonstrates how close and productive was the bond between them. Their temperaments, and the honesty and integrity which characterised both, often brought them into sharp conflict, but they also always showed true tolerance and mutual understanding.

Pfister's *Illusion of a Future*, written in reply to Freud's *The Future of an Illusion*, illustrates the personal courage, critical ability, practised skill, as well as respect for Freud's greatness, with which his theologically and psycho-analytically trained colleague opposed his master. This controversy is an example of how scientific discussion with Freud should be conducted. Difference from Freud does not mean breaking with him. On the contrary, as Goethe said, differing opinions on a subject need part men only when their basic outlook differs. But in this Freud and Pfister were closely akin. At the roots of both lay love of truth, indeed love itself, as the central factor in obtaining an understanding of mankind, a total lack of compromise in relation to the ultimate and highest values, and incorruptibility by praise or blame.

A number of Pfister's works were stimulated by conversation

and correspondence with Freud, and similarly Freud took suggestions from Pfister for his own work. There is, for instance, no doubt that he accepted the most varied suggestions for the technique of child analysis from Pfister's very concrete communications concerning the psycho-analysis of children and young persons at the stage of puberty.

In accordance with Pfister's calling, it was in the pastoral field that his analytic work was most fruitful. It is interesting to note that Freud, who speaks of himself as a 'secular pastoral worker',[1] has an open ear for the technique and experiences of the religious and spiritual pastoral worker Pfister, while the latter emphasises the objectivity of Freud, who described himself as being devoid of religious feeling. In this connection Pfister quotes the letter Freud wrote him in which he said:

In itself psycho-analysis is neither religious nor non-religious, but an impartial tool which both priest and layman can use in the service of the sufferer. I am very much struck by the fact that it never occurred to me how extraordinarily helpful the psycho-analytic method might be in pastoral work, but that is surely accounted for by the remoteness from me, as a wicked pagan, of the whole system of ideas.

Pfister's contributions to the practice of psycho-analysis are contained in numerous publications. Even more important than the written word was the impact of his personality. His thesis that true religion can be a defence against neurosis was not denied by Freud, though he thought that in this loveless world it was a rarity and therefore not a thing not to be depended on.

When he talked about his correspondence with Freud Pfister was full of gratitude, pride and pleasure at the structure on which the two 'architects' had worked over the years. In 1944 he entrusted joint responsibility for its publication to the undersigned, subject to the condition that he also imposed on Anna Freud, namely that nothing should be published that might give offence to any living person.

Heinrich Meng

[1] *Seelsorger*

10

III

In the totally non-religious Freud household Pfister, in his clerical garb and with the manners and behaviour of a pastor, was like a visitor from another planet. In him there was nothing of the almost passionately impatient enthusiasm for science which caused other pioneers of analysis to regard time spent at the family table only as an unwelcome interruption of their theoretical and clinical discussions. On the contrary, his human warmth and enthusiasm, his capacity for taking a lively part in the minor events of the day, enchanted the children of the household, and made him at all times a most welcome guest, a uniquely human figure in his way. To them, as Freud remarked, he was not a holy man, but a kind of Pied Piper of Hamelin, who had only to play on his pipe to gather a whole host of willing young followers behind him.

It was this overflowing of feelings for psycho-analysis to its founder, and from him to his children, that led Pastor Pfister after Freud's death to leave the correspondence to me, 'the daughter of his great benefactor', as he called me, with permission to make use of suitable material, subject to the reservation that nothing should be published that might give offence to any living person.

Anna Freud

THE LETTERS

Dear Dr Pfister,

I cannot content myself with just thanking you for sending me your paper *Wahnvorstellung und Schülerselbstmord.*[1] I must also express my satisfaction that our psychiatric work has been taken up by a minister of religion who has access to the minds of so many young and healthy individuals. Half in jest, but really quite seriously, we often complain that psychoanalysis requires a state of normality for its application and that the organised abnormalities of mental life impose a limitation on it, with the result that the optimum conditions for it exist where it is not needed–*i.e.*, among the healthy. Now it seems to me that this optimum exists in the conditions in which you work.

Your name has often been mentioned to me by our common friend C. G. Jung,[2] and I am glad now to be able to associate a more definite idea with it; and I hope you will not keep your future work from me.

With sincere thanks,
Freud

Berggasse 19,
Vienna IX,
9.2.1909

Dear Dr Pfister,

I have to-day re-read your valuable paper, on which I shall open a discussion to-morrow in our small circle,[3] and I should like to hear more from you on the subject than I can

[1] In *Schweizer Blätter fur Schulgesundheitspflege,* 1909, No. 1
[2] Dr Carl Gustav Jung (1875-1961), Professor of Psychology at Zürich
[3] The 'Wednesday psychology club' which met weekly at Freud's flat

gather from the printed word and say more about it than can be put in a letter. Perhaps the opportunity for such an exchange of ideas will arise. To-day I shall confine myself to throwing light on the difference between your field of activity and the medical, as you can also confirm in Stekel.[1]

The permanent success of psycho-analysis certainly depends on the coincidence of two issues: the obtaining of satisfaction by the release of tension, and sublimation of the sheer instinctual drive. If we generally succeed only with the former, that is to be attributed to a great extent to the human raw material – human beings who have been suffering severely for a long time and expect no moral elevation from the physician, and are often inferior material. In your case they are young persons faced with conflicts of recent date, who are personally drawn towards you and are ready for sublimation, and to sublimation in its most comfortable form, namely the religious. They do not suspect that success with them comes about in your case primarily by the same route as it does with us, by way of erotic transference to yourself. But you are in the fortunate position of being able to lead them to God and bringing about what in this one respect was the happy state of earlier times when religious faith stifled the neuroses. For us this way of disposing of the matter does not exist. Our public, no matter of what racial origin, is irreligious, we are generally thoroughly irreligious ourselves and, as the other ways of sublimation which *we* substitute for religion are too difficult for most patients, our treatment generally results in the seeking out of satisfaction. On top of this there is the fact that we are unable to see anything forbidden or sinful in sexual satisfaction, but regard it as a valuable part of human experience. You are aware that for us the term 'sex' includes what you in your pastoral work call love, and is certainly not restricted to the crude pleasure of the senses. Thus our patients have to find in humanity what we are unable to promise them from above and are unable to

[1] Dr Wilhelm Stekel, Vienna nerve specialist and psycho-analyst, born 1868, died London, 1940

supply them with ourselves. Things are therefore much more difficult for us, and in the resolution of the transference many of our successes come to grief.

In itself psycho-analysis is neither religious nor non-religious, but an impartial tool which both priest and layman can use in the service of the sufferer. I am very much struck by the fact that it never occurred to me how extraordinarily helpful the psycho-analytic method might be in pastoral work, but that is surely accounted for by the remoteness from me, as a wicked pagan, of the whole system of ideas.

Let me express the hope that your interest will not fade if the first phase of striking successes gives way to the familiar second phase in which the difficulties tend to obtrude. After overcoming the latter one attains a feeling of quiet confidence.

I make practically no use of the association technique,[1] and see no advantage in it over my own technique of free association, which has not been fully communicated yet. However, in intractable cases—as I knew and as is confirmed once more from your reports—it is very valuable, and for dealing with psychotic states such as dementia praecox it is indispensable. That is because our neurotics suffer severely and put a high degree of co-operativeness at our disposal.

It is certainly not the least of our friend Jung's services that he has become the source of stimuli such as impelled you to your work. Let us hope that the spark that we keep from going out here by laborious fanning will turn with you into a fire from which we in our turn will be able to fetch a flaming torch.

Yours with grateful thanks,
Freud

[1] The use of reactions to a pattern of stimulus words as devised by C. G. Jung

Zürich,
18.2.1909
Dear Professor,

Your letter has made the pleasure I take in the science initiated by you even greater. It was a great satisfaction to me to gather from your remarks that basically I have correctly understood the application of psycho-analysis to pastoral work. The (ethical) difference between your outlook and mine is perhaps not so great as my calling might suggest. Protestant ethics . . . removed the odium of immorality from sexual relations. For the Reformation was fundamentally nothing but an analysis of Catholic sexual repression, unfortunately a totally inadequate one, hence the anxiety neurosis of church orthodoxy and the concomitant phenomena – the witch trials, political absolutism, the social rigidity of the guild system, etc. We modern Evangelical pastors feel ourselves to be completely Protestant, and we are sure[1] that we are much too little reformed. We are searching for a new land. Our Church leaves us Zürichers complete liberty. In ethical matters we are able to be free thinkers without being heroes. Sexual conditions, particularly in our towns, are full of hypocrisy and therefore of uncleanness. The dreadful combination of monogamy and lies and the plague of prostitution are completely clear and intolerable to us. The ideal of *free* love glows in us too. But what we do not see is how really free love can be combined with marriage. The dividing line between 'free' and 'wild' love is very hard to draw. . . .

We shall be freed from the mass misery of neurosis and vice, not by better theories about the marriage tie, but only by an improvement in social conditions, healthier education, and a healthier outlook on life. In the meantime my only recourse is to put forward the ideal of marriage and leave it to the individual and his conscience to decide how far he will depart from it. The more one abides by the doctrine of Jesus and refrains from judgment and confines oneself quietly and

[1] Word doubtful in the original

18

energetically to fighting one's own battle for the ideal, the easier one makes sublimation to the weak. . . .

Berggasse 19,
Vienna IX,
20.2.1909

Dear Dr Pfister,

I conclude with great pleasure from your letter that our differences begin only at the point at which influencing the thought process by emotional stimuli becomes permissible, and thus amount to no more than a useful variation.

In the historical sense of which you speak I too can call myself a protestant, and in that connection I recall that my friend Professor von Ehrenfels[1] coined the term 'sexual protestants' for us both.

Please do not assume that the ridicule and misunderstandings in the press affect me greatly. There are days when the uniformity of the reactions are somewhat oppressive, but not an hour when I doubt that the insights which you too value (not, I hope, over-value) will get through.

If you receive a small book[2] from me early in March, please accept it as a token of my high appreciation of your efforts and co-operation.

Cordially yours,
Freud

[1] Christian Freiherr von Ehrenfels (1859–1932), Professor of Philosophy in the University of Prague

[2] Presumably *Delusions and Dreams in Jensen's 'Gradiva'*, in *The Complete Psychological Works of Sigmund Freud*, Standard Ed. Vol. IX, p. 3. Hogarth Press, London

Berggasse 19,
Vienna IX,
18.3.1909
Dear Dr Pfister,

Perhaps I cannot better express my thanks for your latest paper[1] in the *Evangelische Freiheit* than by asking you to accept some observations that occurred to me while reading it.

I realised that your situation and public laid you under the necessity of withholding or censoring a great deal. That is always as painful to the author as it is to the understanding reader. The censor cuts into the flesh; what he cuts out is always 'the best thing', as the mocker Heine remarks. At one point, I think, you could have been more outspoken for, after all, ecclesiastical authority cannot object to the human phantasy's taking charge of the messages which it has no hesitation in so obtrusively proclaiming.

In the first dream 'the young lady *jumped into the lake*, I wanted to go after her, but *she kept herself above the water . . . she was immediately* quite dry'.

Dreams with this content, as you certainly have long been aware, are birth dreams. Children come from the water, fetched by the stork. The bit of biological reality behind this is familiar to us all, hence the impulse to give children this piece of information. Thus emerging from the water is equivalent to giving birth. (As a consequence of the indissoluble connection between death and sexuality a poor woman who wishes to commit suicide can do so only by means of a symbolic performance of a sexual phantasy. She goes into the water, *i.e.*, gives birth, or flings herself from a height, *i.e.*, drops,[2] or takes poison, *i.e.*, becomes pregnant. Poisoning as a consequence of morning sickness is equivalent to pregnancy.)

---

[1] O. Pfister, *Ein Fall von Psychoanalytischer Seelsorge und Seelenheilung Evangelische Freiheit*, 1909, Nos. 3–5

[2] The German *niederkommen*, 'to descend', also means (of a woman) 'to be confined'

Because of the ease by which things are represented by their opposite, the symbolisms of child-bearing and being born are often exchanged. In the well-known exposure myths of Sargon of Agade, Moses, Romulus, etc., putting the child out in a basket or in the water means the same; both mean being born. (See in this connection Vol. 5 of *Angewandten*[1] due to appear shortly, Rank's[2] *The Myth of the Birth of the Hero*. Box is *box*,[3] casket, genitals, womb–which takes us to the flood myths.)

In the dream he wanted to hurry to the aid of the young lady who jumped into the water, but she remained afloat and emerged by herself. As this young lady was the Madonna, this incident means he wished to help her to give birth, *i.e.*, to have a child, but she gave birth without male intervention, remained a virgin. Hence the next reference. She immediately became quite dry, in other words the conception was immaculate. The hesitation at the end of the dream, the doubt about her, can only reflect the dreamer's doubt about the Catholic doctrine which he would like to accept, about the possibility of the immaculate conception and virgin birth.

His feeling that there was nothing new in the dream, that he had dreamt it all before, fits in well with the usual interpretations. It is quite common to dream of a landscape and have the feeling that one has been there before. This landscape is always the maternal genitals, which is undoubtedly the place of which one can say with the greatest certainty that one has been there before, because otherwise one would not be alive. It has the same meaning: I have dreamt something of the sort before (I have often had this wish, for the maternal genitals, before). I realise of course that it would not have been so easy for you to include this piece of dream interpretation, even if it had been clear to you, as that about the virgin birth.

Our predecessors in psycho-analysis, the Catholic fathers,

---

[1] *Schriften zur Angewandten Seelenkunde*, Deuticke, Leipzig and Vienna, 1909   [2] Otto Rank, psycho-analyst, 1886–1939
[3] Word in English in the original

did not of course work on the principle of paying a mere minimum of attention to sexual matters, but very explicitly asked for full details. I believe that the truth lies in between, but much nearer the Catholic practice than your proposition.

Your work should soon yield a typical result, as the general lines of religious thinking are laid down in advance in the family. God is equivalent to father, the Madonna is the mother, and the patient himself is no other than Christ.

Evidence of how stimulating your work is is the confession that I could fill another sheet of paper with marginal observations. Just one more point. These case histories have only strengthened my impression that the suggested association technique, though indispensable in cases of dementia praecox, has no special value in the analysis of neurotics, and is in no way preferable to free association. The reactions are no less displaced and, if anything, the spinning out of an idea leads to difficulties.

With warm greetings and wishes for the progress of your excellent work,

Yours,
Freud

Berggasse 19,
Vienna IX,
30.3.1909

Dear Dr Pfister,

Jung left yesterday evening, but I obviously had no complaints about you to make to him, because all you have done is what he and I myself have done, that is to say, published material according to the state of your knowledge at the time and modified it later in accordance with the progress of your knowledge. In so doing we give the uninformed reader enough that is new, and more than he is ready to take. The value of what we write must depend on its containing nothing accepted on authority, but only what can be stated as the direct outcome of our own troublesome labours.

Further work will result in your convincing yourself of the justification of accepting a relatively fixed dream symbolism. I wished only to draw your attention to this; I do not call for any act of faith on your part, but only a readiness to assess the appropriate material in such a sense.

The prospect of your coming here in April gives me great pleasure. Please arrange matters so that you can take an evening meal with the family and then remain with me for an hour (I shall be glad if the hour extends to several). If your visit falls on a Sunday, I shall be able to invite you to lunch and we shall be able to see more of each other.

A chance catarrh of the eyes makes writing difficult for me to-day. I therefore postpone a great deal that I have to say until we have the chance to talk it over.

Yours with cordial greetings,

Freud

Berggasse 19,
Vienna IX,
10.5.1909

Dear Dr Pfister,

The Matterhorn[1] now crowns the pile of unanswered letters on my desk. I gladly accept the small fragment of Switzerland in the symbolic sense you suggest, as homage from the only country in which I feel a man of property, knowing that the hearts and minds of good men there are well disposed towards me. I have no intention of defending myself. I have deliberately set myself up only as an example, but never as a model, let alone an object of veneration.

The Matterhorn can easily be given another and more modest meaning. The proportion of one to 50,000 may be roughly that in which fate fulfils our wishes and we ourselves fulfil our intentions. Incidentally it has struck me how little figures mean to our imagination; I have the greatest difficulty in believing that one would have to put only 50,000 of

---

[1] A silver model which was a present from Pfister

these small objects on top of one another to reach the height of a huge mountain. I should have guessed that more than a million would have been required.

I propose to endow the Matterhorn with yet a third meaning. It reminds me of a remarkable man who came to see me one day, a true servant of God, a man in the very idea of whom I should have had difficulty in believing, in that he feels the need to do spiritual good to everyone he meets. You did good in this way even to me. After your exhortation I asked myself why I did not feel really happy, and I soon found the answer. I renounced the impracticable proposition of getting rich honourably, decided after the loss of a patient not to accept a replacement for him, and since then I have felt well and happy and admit that you were right; and subsequently I have adhered to this principle on no fewer than three occasions. But for your visit and your influence I should never have managed it; my own father complex, as Jung would call it, that is to say, the need to correct my father, would never have permitted it.[1]

I shall give your observations about transference and compensation the consideration they deserve. I think you are right; it is the condition of lasting success. One type of woman in particular refuses any abstract substitute and demands some kind of tangible happiness in life or clings to the transference. They are those of whom the poet says that they have understanding only for 'soup logic with dumpling arguments'.[2]

Now accept my very warm thanks. Go on writing valiantly and keep me informed about your struggles and successes.

With cordial greetings,
Yours,
Freud

[1] Freud's father suffered from financial difficulties
[2] The allusion is to Heine's lines from *Die Wanderratten*:

Im hungrigen Magen Eingang finden
Nur Suppenlogik mit Knodelgründen

Dear Dr Pfister,

Many thanks for the number with the paper by Waldburger.[1] I am not quite clear in my mind about him. Is he of the Förster[2] school? I do not fail to see the repulsive, slimysmeary element in it, but all the same it is a pleasing recognition of you. There is something else I am not clear about. He often assumes the air of having waded in psycho-analysis for years, though it must be an unprecedented novelty to him. But probably these riddles are not worth the trouble of solving.

The news about your innumerable interests and activities are as invigorating as usual. I am not clear what you mean by the Dream Book of Aristides. (Artemidorus?)[3] Meanwhile a Herr Spielmaier has said the first kind words about your work; others will follow. I know that does not matter to you.

My state of well being since your visit persists, I am actually engaged in turning a case history[4] I lectured on at Salzburg[5] into an article for the Year Book.[6]

You too must have been impressed by the great news that Jung is coming with me to Worcester.[7] It changes my whole feeling about the trip and makes it important. I am very curious to see what will come of it all.

At about this time of year I acquire a notable similarity to Columbus. Like him, I long for–land.[8] By that we do not

[1] A. Waldburger, *Psychoanalytische Seelsorge und Moral-Pädagogik*, *Protestantische Monatshefte*, 1909
[2] Professor Friedrich Wilhelm Förster, philosopher and educationist, born Berlin 1869, now resident in the United States
[3] Artemidorus of Daldis, Greek author of *Oneirocritica* (dream interpretations), second century A.D.
[4] *Notes upon a Case of Obsessional Neurosis*, Standard Ed. Vol. X, p. 155
[5] The first psycho-analytic congress, Salzburg, 1908
[6] *Jahrbuch für Psychoanalytische und Psychopathologische Forschungen*
[7] To attend the tenth anniversary celebrations of Clark University, Worcester, Mass., at the invitation of the president, Professor Stanley Hall (1846-1924)
[8] *Land* in German also means 'country'

25

always mean America; this year we have in mind the woods round the Hotel Ammerwald, near Reutte, on the Tirolese-Bavarian border. The children are already making one of those calendar devices they call 'hour-gobblers'. I am able to work out in my head that I still have another four and a half weeks to sit out in Vienna.

Those you singled out for greetings feel very honoured. Sophie–that is your neighbour's name–is now with her mother in Hamburg and is expected back in the middle of the week. My second son has his school-leaving examination to-morrow. I believe him now to be playing cards with his two juniors.

With many cordial greetings,
Yours,
Freud

Berggasse 19,
Vienna IX,
12.7.1909

Dear Dr Pfister,

Just before my departure for Ammerwald, Reutte, Tirol, feeling very tired and fed up with the search for truth (which fortunately will remain the case for only a few weeks), I had the pleasure of receiving your letter, and must thank you for the interesting information about men and events. I am really very ignorant about my predecessors in the interpretation of dreams, and if we ever meet in the next world I shall certainly have a bad reception as a plagiarist. But it is so pleasurable to examine things for oneself at first hand instead of consulting the literature about them.

Honnegger[1] has fathomed me well; the sample shows that the young man has a gift for psycho-analysis. Störring[2] has also made a decent impression on me with his book; it would give me pleasure if you gained influence on him. In Jung's opinion sister complexes play a part in the hostility of his

---

[1] J. Honnegger, *Vorlesung über paranoide Wahnbildung*
[2] Gustav Störring, *Zur kritischen Wurdigung der Freudschen Lehre*

pupil Erismann.[1] If only one could get the better people to realise that all our theories are based on experience (there is no reason, so far as I am concerned, why they should not try to interpret it differently) and not just fabricated out of thin air or thought up over the writing desk. But the latter is what they all really assume, and it throws a remarkable light on their own methods of work. I think you are too sanguine about Förster.[2]

Your good shepherd's optimism causes you to set .your hopes too high. A man reckless enough to proclaim public judgment on a matter of which he has such slight knowledge cannot be brought to see reason by any external influence, but follows the demon he has to follow. . . . The only thing that puts me off your interesting Swede (as he calls himself) is that he does not wish to be considered a member of the 'school'. Is that not snobbishness? Has our 'school' secret signs or rites, does it swear by my words or worship me with incense? Those who share our viewpoint belong *ipso facto* to our school, without any initiation ceremony.

The reason I write to you about family matters is that no visitor since Jung has so much impressed the children and done me so much good.

I send you my sincere greetings and look forward to hearing from you again. Letters will reach me either at the old or new address.

Your devoted

Freud

Ammerswald,

16.8.1909

Dear Dr Pfister,

Yes, you can come and see me at any time, and I am delighted to hear from you before undertaking the journey across the barren waste of waters. You always make one cheerful, because you call into consciousness the things

[1] T. Erismann, author of *Angewandte Psychologie*
[2] See footnote 2, p. 25

which because of the unhappy human disposition are hidden behind small miseries and fleeting cares. I do not know what promises you left behind with my children, because I keep hearing things like next year I'm going with Dr Pfister, I'm going climbing with him, and so on and so forth. I dare not mention your 10,000-foot climb with your son, because it would rouse my boys' blackest envy, they would wish they had a father like you, who could still climb with them instead of being tormented by his Conrad[1] and picking strawberries in the woods down below.

Am I really to intervene with my advice in your work plans? There is no need for you to follow it if other motives get the upper hand. I think the prize should be an entirely secondary consideration. If competing does not hold you up, go ahead and take your chance but, if it disturbs you, drop it. But get the work done straight away and do not wait for years before finishing it. Happy is the wooing that's not long in the doing, so to speak. Only while the first impulse lasts will you be able to do the work with so much freshness and vigour. If you go on working, in a few years' time you will see many things differently and more correctly, you will put individual problems in the foreground and suspect deeper connections, but then you will speak a language intelligible only to our community and therefore make no impact on the majority, while now, in the stage of transition between the traditional and the psycho-analytic way of thinking, you will have the subjective strength to carry the unconverted with you. That, in my opinion, is what you want to do, and the important thing is to provide the stimulus. Incidentally, you must have done an enormous amount of work if you have been able to complete the programme you indicated. Good luck to you!

I am still completely unproductive. This year has taken

[1] [*Footnote by Freud.*] This personification of the body in Spitteler's *Imago* impressed me greatly.

(*Imago*, a novel published in 1906 by the Swiss writer Carl Spitteler (1845–1924)

more out of me than previous years. I do not feel like preparing anything for America. Perhaps contact with Jung and Ferenczi[1] (he too is one of the best) will stimulate something. Fortunately I am no longer so necessary and can gradually shrink into an ornament; perhaps there is a bit of providence in that.

I send you my sincere greetings before the journey, and hope during it to hear a great deal about you from Jung.

Yours,
Freud

Berggasse 19,
Vienna IX,
4.10.1909

Dear Man of God,

A letter from you is one of the best possible things that could be waiting for one on one's return. But do not believe that I believe everything or even a large part of the delightful things that you say to me and about me, *i.e.*, I believe them of you but not of me. I do not deny that it does me good to hear that sort of thing, but after a while I recall my own self-knowledge and become a good deal more modest. What remains behind is the belief that you honestly mean what you say, and the pleasure given by your kind and enthusiastic nature. What I should like would be to win over more such people as yourself, Jung (one must not continue 'and others of the same sort'), but there are not very many.

Many thanks for your news. You really do not need to handle Förster with kid gloves. I look forward to receiving your reply to him soon. Fräulein Kaiser[2] is obviously of the right stuff; I wish her good fortune in her work. One of the most agreeable phantasies is that without our knowing it decent people are finding their way to our ideas and aspirations and then suddenly popping up all over the place. That is what happened in the case of Stanley Hall. Who would

[1] Dr Sandor Ferenczi (1873–1933), founder of the Hungarian Psycho-Analytical Society
[2] F. Kaiser, *Analyse einer Melancholie*, a lecture delivered in Zürich

have imagined that over in America, an hour's train journey from Boston, a worthy old gentleman was sitting and waiting impatiently for the Year Book, reading and understanding everything, and then, as he himself put it, ringing the bell for us? I shall not tell you any more about America, as you have heard it all from Jung, or will.

I shall be very pleased if you will send me as many publications as possible in your field, including hostile publications, or let me know where to lay hands on them. We collect everything bearing on psycho-analysis in the society library.[1]

Finally, I wish to confide to you the information that my wife is determined to spend next summer in Switzerland. Incidentally, she is very ambitious without realising it; I have good reason from my self-analysis for forbidding myself ambition. But it is by no means impossible that in due course we shall seek your advice about a place in Switzerland suitable for such a vast multitude as ourselves to spend a pleasant holiday in. That will of course mean passing through Zürich, an eventuality to which I greatly look forward.

With wàrm and cordial greetings,

Yours,
Freud

Berggasse 19,
Vienna IX,
5.11.1909

Dear Dr Pfister,

I received to-day the September–October number of the *Evangelische Freiheit,* presumably from you, and I thank you very much for it. Förster's article had a very soothing effect on me; I expected something more intelligent and adroit. Where Herr F. condescends to criticise a detail, *e.g., aliquis,*[2] his feebleness is tangible.

---

[1] The library of the Vienna Psycho-Analytical Society
[2] An example in Freud's *Psychopathology of Everyday Life,* Standard Ed. Vol. VI

Now I am eagerly looking forward to your reply, and hope that you will produce as much humour as your opponent wasted emotion. (Incidentally C. F. Meyer's[1] mother and sister were denounced as sexual objects not by me, but by Sadger.[2])

I feel well, and again needed someone to assure me that there was no need for me to drudge and that everything would go by itself, which one is so glad to hear.

With cordial greetings,

Yours,

Freud

Berggasse 19,
Vienna IX,
10.1.1910

Dear Dr Pfister,

The year is still young enough for me to be able to begin this letter by expressing the wish that it may be a deservedly happy one for you. My wish for myself, that in the course of it I may win the friendship of more men such as you, is probably too ambitious to have any prospect of fulfilment.

I can answer your theoretical doubts in accordance with your own inclination. There need have been no shameful or horrible incident, but only subsequent repression made it so. All repressions are of *memories*, not of experiences; at most the latter are repressed in retrospect. With the complexes one must be very careful; indispensable as the idea (of complexes) is in various performances, when one is theorising one should always try to find out what lies behind the complex, not make a frontal attack, which is too vague and inadequate.

I am naturally greatly looking forward to your reply and shall read it with pleasure. I have already admitted my misquotation of the line of Oedipus. On the other hand he[3]

[1] Conrad Ferdinand Meyer (1825–95), Swiss author

[2] *C. F. Meyer, eine pathographisch-psychologische Studie*, by Isidor Sadger, Vienna nerve specialist and psychoanalyst, Bergmann, Wiesbaden, 1908

[3] Forster, see footnote 2, p. 25

31

saddles me with Sadger's work on C. F. Meyer, and at any rate the latter might be a printer's error.

When we meet at Nuremberg[1] I shall talk to you about our plans for the summer and appeal for your aid in the name of big and small. This year we aspire to a place in the blessed area of French Switzerland, at a height of about 3,000 to 3,600 feet, with a good hotel and a beautiful lake (and obviously woods), and later in September we want to go down to the Lake of Geneva. On the way we shall of course take a long rest in Zürich and visit our friend there. The savages are crazy with excitement at the prospect, and even the domesticated ladies are greatly looking forward to it. Perhaps you can advise us about a place. We shall accept the best with gratitude.

I am now writing something about Leonardo da Vinci,[2] though in desultory fashion; I hope you will have an opportunity of reading before the end of the year.

Your cordially devoted
Freud

Many thanks for your good wishes to the family, which they reciprocate.

POSTCARD   *19.1.1910*

Dear Dr Pfister,

Please send me the galleys, I shall gladly give myself the pleasure of reading your work in advance. That does not mean that I renounce the work in presentable dress. Frau C. recently brought me your greetings, and Binswanger[3] and his wife are spending the evening with us this week. All the young people are looking forward to seeing you again and identify you with Switzerland.

Cordially yours,
Freud

---

[1] Where the second psycho-analytic congress was held
[2] *Leonardo da Vinci and a Memory of his Childhood*, Standard Ed. Vol. XI, p. 5
[3] Dr Ludwig Binswanger, Swiss psychiatrist and psycho-analyst

Dear Dr Pfister,

To my unbounded thanks for the galleys, which are now back with you again, I now add a few lines to express my mixed feelings on reading them. Do you want to hear the positive or the negative first? Or a mixture of the two? Well, I admire your ability to write like that, in such a moderate, affable, considerate manner, so factually and so much more for the reader than against your opponent. That is obviously the better way educationally and the more appropriate to your calling. In particular, I thank you for leaving me in the background. I could not write like that, I prefer not writing at all, *i.e.*, I do not write at all. I could write only to free *my* soul, to release *my* affect and, as the latter would not emerge in an edifying manner, and as our opponents would be only too delighted to see me roused, I prefer not answering at all. Just imagine it, the fellow plays the upholder of moral rectitude denouncing evil, thus assuming the prerogative of talking nonsense, parading his ignorance and superficiality, unloading his spleen, distorting and making insinuations. And all this in the name of the higher morality. In face of this I could not restrain myself. But, as I am incapable of artistically modifying my indignation, of giving it an aura pleasurable to others, I hold my peace. I could not lower the temperature in dealing with him.

I hope that you too will not engage further in controversy, either with Förster or with anyone else of his stamp, but will instead use paper and pen for describing your own work. Let them gape, and let us continue along our uphill road.

Your informative letter gave me great pleasure. Last week the Binswangers were here–to call them guests would be too high-flown for the kind of hospitality we dispense. He is correct and honest. I squabbled with him slightly, but cordiality was the stronger feeling, and I like him well. His trace of hesitancy will not hold him back for long. There is something in the material itself which forces one onwards, deeper into sexual symbolism, exclusivity, courage to deal with the unconscious on terms of complete familiarity.

This year's congress will give us the opportunity for long and deep discussions. Also it is to last longer than just one day.

With cordial greetings,

Freud

Berggasse 19,
Vienna IX,
6.3.1910

Dear Dr Pfister,

The news that you will be unable to come to Nuremberg is a disappointment to me, particularly as our Swiss plans are in the melting pot, first because we are unable to settle on a place, and secondly because I have to spend from July 15 to August 15 at Karlsbad. So I am quite upset.

Can you not send something from your prolific output for the essays on applied psychology? I am quite prepared to accept the Zinzendorf,[1] without being intimidated by the homosexuality, if it does not exceed five or six signatures in length (about the length of *Gradiva*). You already know that I want to keep the collection serious and not bellettristic. Please see what you can do for me. I have the feeling that my friends are not giving enough support to this enterprise.

I am now writing a paper on Leonardo da Vinci for the same collection, based on a single childhood phantasy that the man unsuspectingly allowed to come down to us. It will cause plenty of offence, but I write really only for a small circle of friends and followers.

Please also let me know on a postcard whether you have in your possession a copy of the *Theory of Sexuality,*[2] which has been out of print for a long time. It has now appeared in a

[1] O. Pfister, *Die Frommigkeit des Grafen Ludwig von Zinzendorf,* Deuticke, Leipzig and Vienna, 1910
[2] *Three Essays on the Theory of Sexuality,* Standard Ed. Vol. VII, p. 125

second edition, which is so unchanged, however, that there is no need of it if you already have the first.

I cannot face with comfort the idea of life without work; work and the free play of the imagination are for me the same thing, I take no pleasure in anything else. That would be a recipe for happiness but for the appalling thought that productivity is entirely dependent on a sensitive disposition. What would one do when ideas failed or words refused to come? It is impossible not to shudder at the thought. Hence, in spite of all the acceptance of fate which is appropriate to an honest man, I have one quite secret prayer: that I may be spared any wasting away and crippling of my ability to work because of physical deterioration.

In the words of King Macbeth, let us die in harness.

With cordial greetings,

Yours,

Freud

Berggasse 19,
Vienna IX,
17.3.1910

Dear Dr Pfister,

I still have not got over your not coming to Nuremberg. Bleuler[1] is not coming either, and Jung is in America, so that I am trembling about his return. What will happen if my Zürichers desert me?

I accept with great pleasure your artistically excoriated saint.[2] He will be printed immediately after Leonardo and will anger a great many good people, I hope. . . .

Thanks from the whole family for your advice and information. We propose to use it next year because, as we shall not be free until August 15 and do not want to pass through

---

[1] Dr Eugen Bleuler (1857–1939), Professor of Psychiatry in the University of Zürich

[2] Nikolaus Ludwig Zinzendorf, Count of Zinzendorf and Pottendorf, German religious and social reformer (1700–60), founder of the Herrnhut community

Zürich without stopping, making the journey this year would not be worth while. Also the times are too unsettled.

I have, as you admit, done a great deal for love, but experience does not confirm that it lies at the base of everything, unless, as is psychologically correct, hate is included with it. But that immediately makes the world look a much gloomier place.

My cordial greetings. Not being able to end this letter like others this year with the words *auf Wiedersehen* in Nuremberg makes me cross all over again.

Yours,
Freud

POSTCARD   *4.4.1910*

Leonardo has just gone to press and is to appear at the beginning of May. Your Zinzendorf can go the same way directly afterwards. The publisher is very pleased with it.

With cordial greetings,
Yours,
Freud

Berggasse 19,
Vienna IX,
2.5.1910

Dear Dr Pfister,

I am sure you need neither introduction nor notes from me. If anything that might be useful to you occurs to me while reading it, it will be at your disposal, *celà va sans dire.* Your count[1] is now awaited, as my Leonardo will definitely see the light during the glorious month of May.

What you call compensation I include under the concept of sublimation, or the similar but clearer one of reaction-formation, which you will not have missed in the *Worcester*

---

[1] Count Zinzendorf, see p. 34

lectures.[1] The latter are only meagre fare, and are no substitute for an introduction to psycho-analysis. I am therefore panting for your Propaedeutics, for we have nothing to put by its side. Dr Hitschmann[2] here is now working on a synthesis of psycho-analytic theory, intended to be an authoritative compilation of material which is now scattered all over the place and offers the beginner nothing. It also deals with the subject from the medical and historical aspects.

I know nothing about three copies of the anti-Förster. If I received two, one has gone to the society library.

I hope you agree with the Nuremberg decisions and will stand loyally by our Jung. I want him to acquire an authority that will later qualify him for leadership of the whole movement.

This summer we shall (at any rate probably) pick on a seaside-place in Holland, because we do not want to be more than a day's journey from Hamburg, where an eighty-year-old grandmother is producing all sorts of debilities. If all goes well, next year–the twenty-first since a certain event[3]–we shall go to Switzerland and then on to Italy.

With cordial greetings and in expectation of your saintly count.[4]

Yours,
Freud

P.S. Followers in England would be as novel as they would be valuable.

---

[1] These two words in English in the original. *Five Lectures on Psycho-Analysis*, Standard Ed. Vol. XI, p. 3. (Delivered in 1909 at Clark University, Worcester, Mass.)
[2] Dr Eduard Hitschmann (1871–1957), psycho-analyst
[3] The reference is to Freud's marriage
[4] See p. 34

Dear Dr Pfister,

At last Sunday has come, giving me an opportunity to read through your *Analysis of Hate and Reconciliation*.[1] Apart from that, I am looking forward to your worthy count, and shall decide after reading it whether to send it back to you for the Year Book.[2] Its possible predecessor[3] is already in your hands.

You ask me in your kind letter to tell you what I think about your *Analysis* and you put questions to me on the thorny question of transference. I can think of no better way of using this fine evening than discussing these things with you. Which shall I begin with, praise or criticism? You will certainly be more interested in the latter.

Well, then, I think your *Analysis* suffers from the hereditary vice of–virtue; it is the work of too decent a man, who feels himself bound to discretion. Now, these psycho-analytical matters are intelligible only if presented in pretty full and complete detail, just as an analysis really gets going only when the patient descends to minute details from the abstractions which are their surrogate. Thus discretion is incompatible with a satisfactory description of an analysis; to provide the latter one would have to be unscrupulous, give away, betray, behave like an artist who buys paints with his wife's house-keeping money or uses the furniture as firewood to warm the studio for his model. Without a trace of that kind of unscrupulousness the job cannot be done. The information you give is of course perfectly adequate to justify the conclusions you draw–I say that in all sincerity–but the true picture is not conveyed to the reader, who cannot identify himself with it with his unconscious and is therefore in no position to exercise his critical faculties.

[1] O. Pfister, *Analytische Untersuchung über die Psychologie des Hasses und der Versohnung*. *Jahrbuch*, 1910
[2] The *Jahrbuch fur Psychoanalytische und Psychopathologische Forschungen*, edited by Jung
[3] Freud's *Leonardo*, Standard Ed. Vol. XI

My second observation concerns technique. In this matter I am certainly too one-sided; I try to demonstrate that one single technique is the correct one and keep on plodding away at it. You have seen correctly that the association technique is suitable for a first orientation but not for carrying out the treatment, for with each new stimulus word you put to the patient you interrupt him and cut off the flow. The spontaneous production of word series you use in analysis is certainly incomparably better, but it does not give a good picture or clear insights, and it seems to me to save no time. Where the patient is able to produce such a series, he would certainly have been capable of producing whole speeches. This would have been slower only in appearance, and would have produced a clear picture of the resistances into the bargain. The production of word series is only a way of circumventing the resistance, and for that I now have no use whatever; I neglect the complexes for the resistances and try to approach the latter direct. That is the chief characteristic of my present technique which, I think, goes deeper and is a more certain guide than any earlier.

The transference is indeed a cross. The unyielding stubbornness of the illness, because of which we abandoned indirect suggestion and direct hypnotic suggestion, cannot be entirely eliminated by analysis, but can only be diminished, and its relics make their appearance in the transference. These are generally conspicuous enough, and the rules often let one down, but one must be guided by the patient's character and not entirely give up one's personal note. In general, I agree with Stekel that the patient should be kept in sexual abstinence, in unrequited love, which of course is not always possible. The more you let him find love the sooner you will get his complexes, but the smaller is the final success, as he gives up the fulfilments of the complexes only because he can exchange them for the results of the transference. A cure has perhaps been achieved, but the patient has not attained the necessary degree of independence and security against relapse. Now, in this respect things are easier for you than for us physicians, because you can sublimate the transference on to religion and ethics, which is not easy for the invalids of life. Probably you do not need the rigorous resistance technique, for you practise psycho-analysis in the service of religion on young persons from most of whom the full force of sex is still remote.

You see, my dear Dr Pfister, how little my observations have in common with criticism. I assess your work only by our latest requirements, which in any case have not yet reached finality. Your concluding sentences show how much clarification and enrichment current psychology can gain from psycho-analysis.

What is happening to your Propaedeutics to which I am so much looking forward?

You know that Switzerland has turned into Holland for us this year. If I can really get to Switzerland next year, I hope I shall find the split in Zürich healed and Jung the victor over the difficulties that are now being prepared for him.

With cordial greetings from myself and the family,

Yours,
Freud

Berggasse 19,
Vienna IX,
17.6.1910

Dear Dr Pfister,

I have read through your Zinzendorf quickly and with great interest. The result is that I have not the slightest intention of giving it up. It has every conceivable qualification for a number of the Contributions to Applied Psychology.[1] I can see no reason for hiding him.

The independent existence for which he is admirably equipped will be very good for him. I had expected something quite different, of a piquant or scandalous kind, but I now retract all my calumnies of the count. He is an honest

[1] *Schriften zur Angewandten Seelenkunde*

40

poor fool, no more of a fraud than all great men are, according to Fontane.[1]

Your work on him is revealing down to the last detail, effective, and completely convincing to everyone not determined not to be convinced. Some very minor observations. When you talk about sublimations of the libido you sometimes drop into a rather stiff, formal phraseology which will puzzle the uninitiated. You did not emphasise the boy's notably intense sexual disposition but, as in the case of all religious pioneers, that can be assumed. The cult of the wound suggests the finding in *The Interpretation of Dreams* that the female genitals are thought of in infancy as a 'wound'. (I think in the section on infantile material as a source of dreams).[2] Thus the origin is the same as the so brilliantly explained small hole in the side.

In accordance with my abominable principle of taking the excellent for granted, I have nothing else to add.

So you will have to tell Jung that for the first time I am refusing him something.[3] You will have the manuscript back in the next few days. In its present form I think it will be too difficult for the type-setter, there will be a great deal he will not be able to read. Send me the final version soon.

My son Ernst is very proud of your greeting. The book I let the children have is a popular medical book, *Die Gesundheit*, to which I contributed myself.[4] It is quite dry and factual.

With cordial greetings,

Yours,

Freud

[1] Theodor Fontane, German writer (1819–98)
[2] The allusion will be found in Standard Ed. Vol. IV, p. 201
[3] Jung wished to publish the paper on Zinzendorf in the Year Book
[4] See *Psychical (or Mental) Treatment*, Standard Ed. Vol. VII, p. 282

Berggasse 19,
Vienna IX,
19.7.1910

Dear Dr Pfister,

Your Zinzendorf went off the same day to Deuticke, who received it with the gratified remark: 'Something from quite a different circle'. Did he mean the author or the subject?

In your theoretical doubts go quietly into the question of transference and resistance. In the earlier catharsis the transference was taken for granted, rather like the omnipresence of the divine being; Herr X and Frau Y are present, with the Lord as onlooker, but He is taken for granted and so He remains unmentioned. The difficulties begin only when the transference is hostile and negative, and depend on the extent to which it is these things, as it is in the case of most decent neurotics.

With sublimation one is dependent less on one's views than on the patient's capacity. One does what one can.

Your idea of polarisation is excellent. I call it disentangling the conflicts in which our instincts generally make their appearance. It is as if a cook put all the sugar in one corner of the batter and all the salt in the other. Naturally that spoils the dish. A beautiful but not yet completely worked out idea.

With grateful thanks for leaving me the count and best wishes for the summer.

Yours,
Freud

P.S. Pages 9*ff.* seemed familiar to me from the ideas of Jung.

The Hague,
23.7.1910

Dear Dr Pfister,

A letter from you is always an occasion, and to-day I simply cannot go to bed without answering you, for shame would not let me sleep. Just imagine it, the intelligent things you say about the splitting up of the instincts – their polarisation–awaken barely an echo in me and no trace of under-standing. In ten days I have grown quite stupid and perfectly happy about it. But do not be angry at having written all this to me, for your letter remains with me, and the day will come when I shall again be able to understand its contents. One thing I can tell you, and that is that you again do yourself a grave injustice when you talk of the struggle with the elemental; I know that that is the hardest of all, and I know that I am–or rather was–very far from having come to an end of it. How strange it is when of two interlocutors one speaks out of libido cathexis and the other from a situation of withdrawal, just like a lover wooing a frigid beauty.

I hear that you are achieving miracles with the subjects of your investigation, and admire you for it. I also hear that one Förster is praising me to the skies (have I read correctly?) and I hear wonderful things about you.

As for what we are doing, that is to say, myself and two of the boys–the eldest is in the Tirolese mountains–it is not very impressive. We bathe in the sea, wait for the excellent meals, take half-hour trips by train to go and see interesting little Dutch towns, stop occasionally in front of beautiful pictures, and in the evening we play cards with each other. Incidentally I am spending a wicked amount of money, which is very good for my unsubdued complex. We are still alone here, as my wife is with her very frail mother in Hamburg, and my daughters are still with their aunt in Austria. We are all to meet at the Hotel Nordzee, Noordwijk, on August 1, unless the light goes out in Hamburg earlier.

I hope I have not put you off sending me a few more friendly lines during the holidays.

You know how much good they always do me.

Your devoted
Freud

P.S. There is to be a second edition of the first series of the *Collected Papers on the Theory of the Neuroses*,[1] for which I am to write an introduction.

[1] S. Freud, *Sammlung Kleiner Schriften zur Neurosenlehre*, Vienna, 1906

Dear Dr Pfister,

I returned rather hurriedly yesterday from Syracuse–Palermo–Rome to avoid the cholera in Naples, hence the delay; normally I answer your letters more promptly.

From what you say I cannot yet form a very good idea of your gift-of-tongues effort,[1] but I expect you will soon be in a position to reveal all the so-called involuntary actions as the work of complexes. Certainly something can be done with it, first of all a stimulating paper in the *Zentralblatt*, and then all sorts of other things.

As you do me the honour of asking my advice about the writing of the book, let me say frankly that the way to which you feel less drawn seems to me the more appropriate and the more advantageous to the reader. In the present state of our knowledge all the fundamentals, consciousness, emotion, etc., are better left in the semi-darkness from which they stand out so well, while one occupies oneself with the outbuildings, approaches, etc., which are only now becoming perceptible. For that the learner will be very grateful.

Professor G., to whom you in your humanitarianism were much too kind, now claims in a criticism of the Year Book in the Journal of Psychology (and Physiology of the Sense Organs) that you pronounced him to be free of complexes. He does not mention you by name, but I know that he means you, because he told us the same thing. As I believe the fellow to be incapable of speaking the truth, I assume that what he says in this case is from three quarters to five quarters false too.

I too begin my working year on October 1, and hope that it will bring all of us no less progress and friendship than the last.

Cordially yours,
Freud

Deuticke had delayed your Count somewhat, but promises to launch him very soon.

[1] O. Pfister, *Die psychologische Enträtselung der religiösen Glossolalie und der automatischen Kryptographie*, Deuticke, 1912

44

My dear Dr Pfister,
I hope you have already consoled yourself about Sch. [*sic.*][1] The warning cannot do any harm. About L. I know nothing yet. The battle is now really warming up, and single leadership is really necessary. If Jung were at home, I should have to write to him daily. I know where he is from the picture postcards he sends me, but not when he is returning.

I have at last 'made nerve contact'[2] with Bleuler and received a long letter from him in reply. He seems to be satisfied with my step and wants a personal discussion. Perhaps I shall arrange to come to Zürich over Christmas if he does not mind the holiday's being disturbed. His arguments, it seems to me, are superficial. The 'intolerant sect' allegation is easy to refute; the intolerance is really not on our side. If my friends are now ready to accept what I say, that is only because they have found so much of it to be borne out, and a natural compensation for the incredulity which I encountered for ten years. Whether a continuation of the correspondence with Bleuler will lead to anything I cannot judge. In any case the criticism of his negativism in the *Korrespondenzblatt*[3] was not entirely appropriate. The place for a controversy of this kind is the scientific journal, the new *Zentralblatt* if the Year Book is excluded as being edited by him. Publishing it in the *Korrespondenzblatt* associates him with other opponents who are exposed to kicks there. There is plenty of occasion now for internal controversy, which will be continually renewed, but controversy with the outside world distracts attention. Building the temple with one hand and with the other .

[1] Freud was at this time writing the Schreber case history. Note reference to paranoia on next page and p. 47
[2] An expression taken from Daniel Paul Schreber's *Denkwürdigkeiten eines Nervenkranken*
[3] The *Korrespondenzblatt*, founded by the International Psycho-Analytical Association in 1910, was later merged with the *Zentralblatt*

wielding weapons against those who would destroy it – strikes me as a reminiscence from Jewish history.

I am greatly looking forward to your paper on the gift of tongues. I am wrestling with the problem of paranoia and making only slow progress. There is not enough time, one has to earn one's daily bread, but the work continually provides new stimulus.

With cordial greetings,
Freud

Many thanks for the Zinzendorf. Actually it is now my *sixth* copy.

Berggasse 19,
Vienna IX,
20.1.1911

Dear Dr Pfister,

I am several letters deep in your debt, and have been drawing extensively on the indulgence you show for my complicated circumstances. Perhaps your repeated question about my technical rules and maxims may have played a part in my dilatoriness, because I obviously do not like being reminded of them. Part of the work has been finished for eighteen months, but the whole is not yet ripe, and the author is very tired. So I cannot promise anything for a long time to come. Till then techniques will have to grow wild.

During the past fortnight we have been preoccupied by my son's accident; he broke his thigh while skiing on the Schneeberg, was brought down with difficulty, and is now in a sanatorium. But things are taking their regular course and apparently will leave few serious consequences behind.

I was delighted by the success of our interview in Munich. The refreshment gained there has faded away again. It cannot be helped. In the autumn I hope at last to see my Zürich friends at leisure again. In the meantime I shall certainly see a lot of your literary projects in finished form.

I send you my cordial greetings, bid you farewell for the

46

moment, and commend myself, not to your forbearance from correspondence, but only to your indulgence.

Your devoted
Freud

Berggasse 19,
Vienna IX,
26.2.1911
Dear Dr Pfister,

What an abundance of work in all stages of development and completion. I knew nothing of course about your London contacts. Things now seem to be moving in England; I recently received an invitation to be put up as corresponding member of the Society for Psychical Research.

As for your nun now quartered with the *Zentralblatt*,[1] I should have published her long ago, but I seldom actively intervene, there is a shortage of space as it is, and the two editors always have special wishes of their own. But I shall press them. I have all sorts of things in mind for the *Zentralblatt* which are not yet ready to be talked about.

That you should be holding anything back in expectation of my rules and maxims upsets me greatly. I feel so far away from them, and suspect that their turn will not come for years. The Paranoia[2] will be appearing in the next Year Book, and in the summer (at Karlsbad) I hope to be able to work on a part of the big synthesis (vicissitudes of the libido)[3] which interests me most at present. So you will have to rely on your own resources, the maxims are not yet ripe. Thirst cannot wait so long as that.

In Vienna there has been a small crisis of which I have not yet told Jung. Adler[4] and Stekel have resigned, and next

---

[1] O. Pfister, *Hysterie und Mystik bei Margarethe Ebner (1291–1351)*, *Zentralblatt*, 1911, Vol. I

[2] The Schreber analysis. Standard Ed. Vol. XII

[3] Presumably *Instincts and their Vicissitudes*, Standard Ed. Vol. XIV, p. 111

[4] Dr Alfred Adler (1870–1937), founder of Individual Psychology

47

Wednesday I am letting myself be elected president.[1] (A parallel would be if Bleuler assumed the presidency in Zürich.) Adler's theories were departing too far from the right path, and it was time to make a stand against them. He forgets the saying of the apostle Paul the exact words of which you know better than I: 'And I know that ye have not love in you.' He has created for himself a world system without love, and I am in the process of carrying out on him the revenge of the offended goddess Libido. I have always made it my principle to be tolerant and not to exercise authority, but in practice it does not always work. It is like cars and pedestrians. When I began going about by car I got just as angry at the carelessness of pedestrians as I used to be at the recklessness of drivers.

Yes, it is true, this time I am going to give myself a treat. I shall be coming to Zürich in the second half of September with my wife, and staying until the congress. This time you are not to play truant from the congress. The 'elf'[2] is once more very much in need of the cure at Karlsbad. My reckless boy's leg is healing well, my eldest, who is hardly mine any more, is fine, the rest are thriving. A sudden drop in my practice is giving me almost more leisure than I wanted after working at full pressure for four months. However, such reliefs from work do not lead to any productivity with me; I have to patch together the third edition of *The Interpretation of Dreams*.

With best wishes and thanks for your kind words,

Your devoted
Freud

Berggasse 19,
Vienna IX,
20.4.1911

Dear Dr Pfister,

How delightful of you to remember me at Easter. Thank you for the news about your work and the interest it is

[1] Of the Vienna Psycho-Analytical Society
[2] Freud's daughter Sophie

48

rousing. I knew nothing about your contacts with Meumann;[1] nowadays I read nothing that is not sent to me. As for your difficulties with Siebeck, I should first try reasoning with him, as a theological publisher has obvious advantages for you. But you can add that you have no intention of putting pressure on him, as you are not incommoded by the lack of an alternative publisher. Deuticke, when I sounded him on the matter, said that he would be more than willing to take your book, though he too thinks you should try a theological publisher first. So you have nothing to worry about.

You take a kinder view of events in Vienna than they deserve. It is really uncomfortable and disagreeable. Certainly the father complex has come into play, but from the standpoint that father is not doing enough for them. Criticism of the impotent father. In fact my capacity to distribute patients has declined considerably in this year of continual agitation. With Stekel there will probably be a reconcilation; he is incorrigible, but fundamentally decent, and he has done great services to psycho-analysis. But the other one will go overboard.

Physically I am very well, and in that state unfortunately I am always rather lazy. On July 8 I am to go to Karlsbad, for which my wife left with the little (*i.e.*, middle) girl yesterday. In the autumn I shall be visiting you all in Zürich, but cannot yet say whether it will be before or at the time of the congress. This year you must attend it; that will not prevent our spending a few agreeable hours together in your city apart from that.

Your young son is well, I hope?

With cordial greetings from
Yours,
Freud

[1] E. Meumann, author of *Über Lesen und Schreiben im Traume*, 1909

Dear Dr Pfister,

Many thanks for telling me your plans. The great difficulty,
I think, will arise in fitting the complex-psychology into the
psycho-analysis, for the distinctive marks of their divergent
origin have by no means been eliminated. Your attempt at a
synthesis will be keenly awaited and eagerly examined. So
go ahead, and in no circumstances let yourself be held up for
long by Siebeck; I almost have the impression that you will
after all have to go to Deuticke, who will zealously promote
sales in the circles that concern you.

I find it very intelligible that we attach so little value to
appearances at congresses.[1] Public debate of psycho-analysis
is hardly possible; one does not share common ground, and
against the lurking affects nothing can be done. Psycho-
analysis is a deep-going movement, and public debates are
bound to be as useless as the theological disputations of the
time of the Reformation.

In the discussion you sent to me about Count Zinzendorf
your openness and clarity stood out magnificently against the
fulsome reserve of your opponents. The latter is certainly not
the worst that one comes up against, but you see how in discussions of this kind you merely talk past each other. . . .

Our congress, which you must not miss, does not include a
Sunday. The dates are September 21 and 22.

With cordial greetings,

Yours,

Freud

[1] *I.e.*, general psychiatric congresses

Dear Dr Pfister,

For Munich read Weimar,[1] where I hope to see you in the shadow of our greatness. Many thanks for the papers you have sent me. The controversial matter is extremely interesting. In the last there is a large dose of sweet-tasting theological poison, which is more appetising, but what does he mean by 'east European students just sprung from a south Russian ghetto'? The cloven hoof.

The *Zentralblatt* has now got rid of one editor (Adler) and, as I am again on very good terms with Stekel, will now be much more subject to my influence. We did not have any exaggerated idea of the value of the contributions to which you object – no doubt Epstein's and Luzenberger's[2] – but politics spoil everything, characters and *Zentralblätter* alike. If we had declined these first contributions, we should have made the authors unhappy and turned them into enemies. . . .

I am counting the days until July 9, and in the meantime getting more dull-witted every day. When I complain about this, the answer I get is: No wonder. There are few wonders.

Ernst, who was your favourite and might easily have been ours, is now taking his school-leaving examination while suffering from an intestinal ulcer and feeling unwell. He wants to be an architect. I do not know whether I should agree.

With cordial greetings,

Your devoted,

Freud

[1] The third psycho-analytic congress held at Weimar was originally to have been held at Munich

[2] D. Epstein, *Beitrag zur Psychopatholigie des Alltagslebens,* and A. Luzenberger, *Psychoanalyse in einem Fall von Errotungsangst als Beitrag zur Psychologie des Schamgefuhls, Zentralblatt,* 1911

Dear Dr Pfister,

As you are letting me see the proofs of your Gift of Tongues, I must show myself worthy of the honour and pick some holes in it, thus depriving myself of the pleasure of reading it straight through.

I received to-day the first set of galleys (up to 288), and my critical eye finds your interpretation of the vision of the devil (p. 285) too simple, too facile. The devil's wearing the innocent young girl's nose on his face as the 'visible sign of his slander' is too tamely expressed and too simply explained. Let us make a more plausible assumption, one which fits in better with our knowledge, and say that such a vision is not a simple wish-picture but the product of several conflicting stimuli with one of them predominating. In that case the devil would be a mixed formation, really standing also for the girl, and his nakedness is even better explained as a means of seduction than as a sign of her humiliation. Without this there is no explanation of why the devil should have got the girl's certainly very pretty little nose as recompense for his slanderous deed. The pious are not usually as generous as that in their ravings.

Incidentally, the symbolic representation of the genitals by the nose will – with the aid of the infantile element – certainly have been the reason why the nose was chosen from the girl's body. In short, the vision does not seem to me to have been fully interpreted, and it might be as well to express yourself more cautiously about it, or with some indication of the other probabilities. The beginning of the analysis of the crazy 'speaking with tongues' is terribly amusing.

With cordial greetings,

Yours,

Freud

Karlsbad,
12.7.1911

Dear Dr Pfister,

. . . You seem to have taken a liking to Sachs,[1] which pleases me greatly. I hope this year's congress will lead to many good contacts. I am counting on seeing you during the week beforehand.

Do not fritter yourself away on reports, we expect something different from you.

I have been here since the ninth inst., and am still very exhausted and quite incapable of work. I have a Dutch pupil here for company in the evening.

With best wishes for your holiday.

Your cordially devoted
Freud

Berggasse 19,
Vienna IX,
14.12.1911

Dear Dr Pfister,

I have had a gloomy day myself to-day and shall cheer myself up by having a few words with you. . . .

I have prodded the editors of *Psyche* (or *Imago*)[2] not to omit the paper on krypterga.[3]

Who is the *Messmer* you mention in your letter? Surely not the venerable father of mesmerism, who spelled his name with one S fewer? You write about him as though I knew him. Is vile senility causing my memory to fail?

I find it a great nuisance that the new journal wants something from me, an introductory article to boot. I am finding the psychogenesis of religion very hard going, and with the feeble powers at my disposal I shall have a job to finish it in

[1] Dr Hanns Sachs (1881–1947), psycho-analyst and author of *Freud, Master and Friend*, London, 1950

[2] *Zeitschrift zur Anwendung der Psychoanalyse auf die Geisteswissenschaften*

[3] O. Pfister, *Kryptographie und unbewusstes Vexierbild bein Normalen*, *Jahrbuch*, 1913

53

time. I cannot bear working to a date-line. It ceases to be a pleasure and becomes just like the rest of the daily grind.

I am delighted that you stood up to Bleuler. You are not a man who does things by halves. I am always delighted to see that confirmed. When I come to Zürich soon let us go on an outing together to the Ufenau and take with us C. F. Meyer's little book.[1] Then you shall read me the lines:

> *Mich reut, ich streu mir Aschen auf das Haupt,*
> *Dass nicht ich fester noch an Sieg geglaubt!*
> *Mich reut, ich beicht' es mit zerknirschtem Sinn,*
> *Dass nicht ich Hutten stets gewesen bin!*[2]

. . . I am still too dull and stupid to take up any more of your time, so here are my best wishes, and let me hear from you again soon.

Yours,
Freud

Berggasse 19,
Vienna IX,
9.2.1912

Dear Dr Pfister,

I understand your displeasure at perpetually writing expository articles and self-eulogies, and certainly cannot recommend you to continue with the malpractice. But your colleagues would certainly take a refusal very much amiss, so I suppose you will have to give them something. I can understand that you do not want to go alone; perhaps someone will turn up who will accompany you and gladly do battle at your side. I was delighted at all the news about your work.

I know little about K., as my news from your city has recently been meagre. I have no memory of him as a pupil (1); he may have heard one or more of my lectures. I cannot remember all those who put down their names for them in all

---

[1] *Huttens letzte Tage*

[2] I bewail that I did not believe still more firmly in victory, I strew ashes on my head. I bewail, I confess with contrition, that I have not always been Hutten

these years. All the same, a Swiss would probably have struck me, but he certainly had no closer contact with me than that.

To-day I read in proof your excellent paper for *Imago*,[1] and as its host I must ask you to refer to me in more modest terms. I know what you mean, and that sort of thing only excites ridicule among our opponents.

With the patients at home here things are going better than expected. The others are well and they all send you their greetings through

Your cordially devoted

Freud

Berggasse 19,
Vienna IX,
2.5.1912

Dear Dr Pfister,

Forgive my candid explanation for replying by return of post. To-day I have been having a headache, and am not yet in a fit state to attend to my other affairs.

In regard to your doubts about where to place the book to which we are all looking forward, personally I should vote for Messmer's series[2] and against Deuticke, though in the last resort it is not very important which you choose. I know that Deuticke always makes difficulties, and complains about the sales of Hitschmann,[3] for instance. But he will certainly take your book.[4] On the other hand I am attracted by the prospect of gaining a new and not yet opened-up circle of readers in the field of education, while none of us would be put off buying the book by its inclusion in the series. Our

[1] O. Pfister, *Anwendung der Psychoanalyse in der Pädagogik und Seelsorge*, *Imago*, 1912

[2] *Berner Seminarblätter*, edited by Oskar Messmer

[3] Eduard Hitschmann, *Freuds Neurosenlehre nach ihrem gegenwärtigen Stand*, Deuticke, 1911

[4] O. Pfister, *Die psychoanalytische Methode—erfahrungswissenschaftlisch-systematische Darstellung*, Klinkhardt, 1913. English version, *The Psycho-Analytic Method*, Kegan Paul, London, 1917

capacity for expansion in the medical profession is unfortunately very limited, and it is important to secure a footing elsewhere where we can.

I am always delighted when you write so cheerfully and have had no unfriendly experiences.

Several passages in your letter have caused me to note with regret that our contacts with Zürich are not so close as they might be. Thus, for example, I know nothing about any answer of Bleuler's to Kronfeld's piece.[1] I could hardly back the 'pamphlet of the six doctors' against K. because this is the first I have heard of it; I assume it to be identical with the reply planned by Maeder.[2] If Jung were to obtain the professorship without the administrative duties, it would of course be a huge gain for us, but I think that he himself regards it as improbable. A few centuries ago we should have prescribed days of prayer for the fulfilment of our wishes, but nowadays all we can do is wait.

My next effort in the third number of *Imago* will deal with taboo, sketchily, of course. One could fill volumes with all the material available.

I send you my cordial greetings and hope to hear again from you soon.

Yours,
Freud

Berggasse 19,
Vienna IX,
4.7.1912

Dear Dr Pfister,

Many thanks for your letter and the account of your lecture. I attribute to your direct influence a very satisfactory letter from Maeder about the point in question.

It is a pity that you did not meet or speak to Jung. You

---

[1] Arthur Kronfeld, *Über die psychologischen Theorien Freuds und verwandte Anschauungen*, 1912

[2] Alphonse Maeder, Swiss psycho-analyst

could have told him from me that he is at perfect liberty to develop views divergent from mine, and that I ask him to do so without a bad conscience.

A big book by Rank on the incest problem has appeared,[1] and I am very proud of the dedication. I shall be very glad to see your work in print.

With cordial greetings and good wishes,

Your devoted
Freud

Bozen,
2.9.1912

Dear Dr Pfister,

I am compelled to ask you to do me a favour. We – that is to say, Ferenczi and I – intended, after staying in these parts for a short time, to go and see Professor Jones[2] in London, and he has already booked rooms for us. But now my eldest daughter has suddenly been taken ill, still in connection with the unsuccessful operation she had years ago. I am returning to Vienna to-day, can make no definite plans at the moment and, in view of the uncertainty of the situation, shall not be able to go to England as arranged on September 8.

Jones is attending the psychotherapeutic congress in Zürich, but I do not know his address. So I am asking you to be so kind as to seek him out and to tell him the contents of this letter, so that he will be able to cancel the room reservations. Please tell him not to count on my being able to go to London and ask him to write to me in Vienna.

Thanking you in anticipation for your trouble,

Your devoted
Freud

[1] Otto Rank, *Das Inzest-Motiv in Dichtung und Sage; Grundzüge einer Psychologie des dichterischen Schaffens*, Deuticke, 1912
[2] Dr Ernest Jones (1879–1958), founder of the British Psycho-Analytical Society and Freud's biographer

Berggasse 19,
Vienna IX,
9.12.1912

Dear Dr Pfister,

A letter came from you to-day with your last letter still un-answered. I realise that I was put out by your unsatisfactory news. That makes me all the more pleased at your good news in the scientific field, and in particular the fact that your book is so far advanced. I shall be delighted to write you an intro-duction on the lines you ask.

In regard to your production analysis, I should like to sug-gest that you leave it with Imago and make a concession to the publisher, for whom things are not easy, by reducing your demands for illustrations. I already have two papers (by Maeder and Hug[1]), and my original publisher Deuticke is getting restive. The 1913 Year Book is, as you know, always open to you.

We have finished with Bergmann.[2] Jung settled that very well. In January we shall have our journal again in a new guise, and I hope we shall find it satisfactory.

Naturally I am very pleased at your opposition to Jung's innovations, but do not expect me to write anything against him. My disagreement is too obvious to make any impression. But I think he will receive a great deal of criticism from most of the leading analysts. So you will not be isolated in this purely internal and objective battle. I wonder what sort of technique he uses to arrive at such views.

All are well here, but the possibility of war keeps us on tenterhooks.

With my cordial greetings,

Yours,

Freud

[1] Hermine von Hug-Hellmuth, *Aus dem Seelenleben des Kindes*, Deuticke, 1913
[2] The Bergmann Verlag of Wiesbaden, the first publisher of the *Zentralblatt*

Dear Dr Pfister,

Many thanks for your New Year greetings. As we all attach importance to time-limits, let me express the hope that you will finish your book this year.

You and Messmer will be pleased at the firmness with which I propose to defend the rights of educationists to analysis.

In the matter of the libido, there is no reason why you should allow your own view to be overruled. Open your eyes and see for yourself. I am not in any doubt that this 'modification' by your fellow-countrymen is no advance in the direction of truth. The argument that they deduce from the Jones case sounds very strange to me. (Incidentally, as you correctly surmise, it had no influence on Jones himself.) I have myself analysed and cured several cases of real incest (of the most severe kind), and was no more able then than now to deduce from them any argument against the real meaning of incest. Or has knowledge of repression already died out in Zürich? That would explain a great deal, and also revive a lot of old puzzles.

Jung's behaviour in the case of our Frau H. was very ambiguous, but on principle I made no detail of the affair a *casus belli*. He would have spared himself the severe conflict of which you write if only he had not preferred to imagine himself in possession of the secret of curing her *cito et jucunde*. I am inclined to think that he had never had the opportunity of dealing with a case of such intensity and had no idea of the difficulties involved. Do not have too much confidence in a lasting personal agreement between me and Jung. He demands too much of me, and I am retreating from my overestimation of him. It will be sufficient if the unity of the association is maintained.

With cordial greetings,
Yours,
Freud

Berggasse 19,
Vienna IX,
18.2.1913

Dear Dr Pfister,

Herewith my effort,[1] born on a stupid day, but I do not make so bold as to wait for a cleverer one. Tell me what you would like to have altered and let me correct the first galley myself. The firmness of my attitude will please you, but that has always been what I thought in the matter.

With cordial greetings,

Yours,

Freud

Berggasse 19,
Vienna IX,
11.3.1913

Dear Dr Pfister,

My congratulations on having finished your book. I hope that in my judgment of it I shall once more see eye to eye with Jung. Keller's[2] attitude does not surprise me, it corresponds to what I thought of him.

With the Hirschfeld publishing firm – if I am to judge by the proprietor's wife – things will go smoothly. A word in your ear about your translator. I know L. myself, he is a wholly inadequate, wild individual; actually he is a complete ass. Unless he has greatly altered in the meantime, I should entrust no translation to him. But there is a prospect of my finding a translator for you here with whom you should be satisfied. I suggest that you send me the galleys one by one as soon as you receive them. I shall see whether the idea is practicable and let you know as soon as possible.

I have just had to do an unwanted job, a kind of introduction to psycho-analysis for *Scientia;*[3] I did it, not wishing to

[1] The introduction to Pfister's book, see p. 55
[2] The reference is presumably to A. Keller's paper *Ruhige Erwägungen im Kampfe um die Psychoanalyse, Kirchenblatt,* Switzerland, 1912
[3] *The Claims of Psycho-Analysis to Scientific Interest,* Standard Ed. Vol. XIII, p. 163

refuse in view of the admirable character of that international journal. Apart from that, I am looking forward to Easter, which I am going to spend in Venice with my small and now only daughter.

The business advice for which you ask me you had better get from your publisher. Not much good generally comes of translations. . . .

With cordial greeting,

Yours,

Freud

(No letters have survived between the above and that dated September 10, 1918.)

Berggasse 19,
Vienna IX,
9.10.1918

Dear Dr Pfister,

I have now read through your little book[1] and I can well believe the pleasure with which you wrote it. It has a gladdening warmth and demonstrates all the fine qualities which we so value in you; your enthusiasm, your integrity, and love of humanity, your courage and candour, your understanding and also—your optimism.

It will undoubtedly render us good service, if we are to mention such practical considerations; as you know, we generally pay little regard to them.

Well, praise can always be brief, but criticism has to be more long-winded. One thing I dislike is your objection to my 'sexual theory and my ethics'. The latter I grant you; ethics are remote from me, and you are a minister of religion. I do not break my head very much about good and evil, but I have found little that is 'good' about human beings on the whole. In my experience most of them are trash, no matter

---

[1] Presumably O. Pfister, *Was bietet die Psychoanalyse dem Erzieher?* Leipzig, 1917. (*Psycho-Analysis in the Service of Education*, Henry Kimpton, London, 1922)

61

whether they publicly subscribe to this or that ethical doctrine or to none at all. That is something that you cannot say aloud, or perhaps even think, though your experiences of life can hardly have been different from mine. If we are to talk of ethics, I subscribe to a high ideal from which most of the human beings I have come across depart most lamentably.

But the sexual theory? Why on earth do you dispute the splitting up of the sex instinct into its component parts which analysis imposes on us every day? Your arguments against this are really not very strong. Do you not see that the multiplicity of these components derives from the multiplicity of the organs, all of which are erotogenic, *i.e.*, fundamentally all aspire to reproduce themselves in the future organism? And has the fact that all the organs combine to form a living unit, all influencing, aiding or checking one another and remaining dependent on one another even in the process of their development, prevented the anatomists from studying and describing them separately? Or has it prevented the therapists from dealing with a single organ which has become the main site of an agent or process of disease? It may well be that in internal therapy this correlation of the organs has often been forgotten, but in separating out the individual instincts psycho-analysis aims at not losing from sight the interdependence of instinctual life. In science one must take apart before one can put together. It looks to me as if you want a synthesis without a previous analysis. In the technique of psycho-analysis there is no need of any special synthetic work; the individual does that for himself better than we can.

That applies to all the instincts in so far as we can separate them out. But in your little book you do not deal quite correctly with the sexual instincts. You nowhere say that these really have a closer connection with and a greater importance – not for mental life as a whole, though that is what it comes to – but for the development of neurosis; and that that is because of their conservative nature, their closer connection with the unconscious, the pleasure principle and, as a consequence of the peculiarities of their process of development, even with cultural standards. I think that the relics of your resistance to sexuality must have crept into this. Try and revise that part of yourself.

As for the possibility of sublimation to religion, therapeutically I can only envy you. But the beauty of religion certainly does not belong to psycho-analysis. It is natural that at this point in therapy our ways should part, and so it can remain. Incidentally, why was it that none of all the pious ever discovered psycho-analysis? Why did it have to wait for a completely godless Jew?

With cordial greetings from
Your old friend
Freud

PFISTER TO FREUD   *Zürich,*
29.10.1918

. . . Finally you ask why psycho-analysis was not discovered by any of the pious, but by an atheist Jew. The answer obviously is that piety is not the same as genius for discovery and that most of the pious did not have it in them to make such discoveries. Moreover, in the first place you are no Jew, which to me, in view of my unbounded admiration for Amos, Isaiah, Jeremiah, and the author of Job and Ecclesiastes, is a matter of profound regret, and in the second place you are not godless, for he who lives the truth lives in God, and he who strives for the freeing of love 'dwelleth in God' (First Epistle of John, iv, 16). If you raised to your consciousness and fully felt your place in the great design, which to me is as necessary as the synthesis of the notes is to a Beethoven symphony, I should say of you: A better Christian there never was. . . .

Dear Dr Pfister,

Nothing has gone astray. The explanation of my disgraceful failure to answer your last letter is very complicated. In the first place, I was very interested in your proposal to examine my relations to positivism, and proposed to write to you about that at length. Secondly, I was annoyed at the scant success of my effort to put you right in the matter of sexual theory, and proposed to wait until the affect had died down. And then something happened which for a long time took away the desire to write, that is, you know that a great many things have been happening with us of a kind capable of gripping and upsetting one, but one direct consequence of these great convulsions struck me particularly hard.

My son Ernst went off on student's leave to Munich to qualify, and one day at the beginning of the collapse my son Oliver came home from Hungary safe and sound. But my eldest son did not come back and did not write, and when he did not turn up in the mass of returning men we had to assume that something had happened to him. Slowly the darkness cleared. First of all we heard that his regiment was one of those which had been taken prisoner during the last few days of the war—some said actually after the conclusion of the armistice. Had he been taken prisoner with his unit? Was he one of those who escaped and had been shot down by his own side, or by the now hostile population? One could suspect what one liked, according to one's mood. At last, on November 21, a postcard (its predecessors had gone astray) arrived from him from an Italian field hospital, saying he was much better and would soon be taken away. A card received by a friend of his on the same day spoke of great dangers escaped and severe ordeals. But why was he in hospital? Had he had an accident? Had he been wounded, or taken ill? Of course I wrote to him at once and, through Dr Sachs's good offices, to the Red Cross. I do not think he has heard from us yet. Not till four weeks later did another card come from him, dated November 30, telling us that he had been taken prisoner unhurt and 'after absolutely incredible hardships' had gone down with a fever and was then (*i.e.*, at the end of November) being well cared for in a convalescence hospital at Teramo (Abruzzi). We still do not know where he is now, or whether he has heard from us, but we are glad that it is nothing more serious. Superfluous horror, now that the fighting has long since stopped.

Thus your letter received to-day exhorts me no longer to be deflected from writing to you. I thank you very much indeed for your invitation to Switzerland, just as I have thanked Jones for his invitation, which I received through a different channel. The demonstration of such friendly feelings does one good, even though one cannot take advantage of them. Of at least six reasons which stand in the way of accepting such kind offers I shall mention only one. Anyone who now leaves German Austria must leave behind 50-75 per cent of his property. Freedom of movement is eliminated by the ban on tax evasion.

Conditions in Vienna are undeniably very bad, and the future will perhaps be even worse. With us personally things are not bad; with touching fanaticism our Hungarian friends send us provisions of all sorts.

The big endowment for psycho-analytic purposes which a Budapest follower (Dr Anton von Freund) has put at my disposal since the congress on September 29 is to be used to found a psycho-analytic publishing house. Rank is in charge of this enterprise, which began work to-day. We shall publish, not only our journals, but also books, the first of which is to be the sixth edition of the *Everyday Life*. We shall certainly include you among our authors.

As a consequence of setting up this enterprise we have little or nothing left over for other purposes. So I have been embarrassed about how to answer Johann Nohl,[1] whose

[1] Hermann Nohl, Swiss educationist, author of *Die Fruchtbarkeit der Psychoanalyse fur Ethik und Religion, Schweizerland*, 1916

works I too very much liked. On top of this limitation there is the tremendous depreciation of our currency. Can I suggest that a respected colleague should accept 300 francs? That would be equivalent to 1,000 of our crowns, which were once worth 1,050 francs.

I have to-day ordered Heller[1] to send you the fourth volume of my *Collection*.[2] I shall be glad to receive your English book in return. Communications with Switzerland are again open. I hope to hear soon again from you and your new group.

With cordial greetings,

Yours,

Freud

Berggasse 19,
Vienna IX,
24.1.1919

Dear Dr Pfister,

In view of your inquiry I reply by return of post. I think it very satisfactory that you are undertaking the analysis of O., and also hope that as a result you will revise your somewhat heretical views about the constitution and significance of the sex instinct.

My son Martin (Lieutenant, F.A.R. 4/3, Field Post Office 646) recently sent us a telegram from Genoa. Your offer is very kind, but I do not know what you can do for him or for us.

Rank, with whom I have discussed it all, will be writing to you direct about the publishing matter. He has himself been thinking of going to Switzerland if prospects of useful co-operation offer. Speaking generally, we need, not another psycho-analytic publishing house, whose interests would be purely commercial, but branches in non-German-speaking countries. We have resources sufficient to enable us to print everything that seems to us worth while, and no interest

---

[1] Hugo Heller, Vienna bookseller and publisher
[2] *Sammlung Kleiner Schriften zur Neurosenlehre*, Vol. IV, 1918

in seeing the market flooded with inferior psycho-analytic wares.

Your English book is certain of a good reception. I have had Herr Nohl sent through a bank the 1,000 crowns (not as advance but as outright payment), but perhaps it will take some time for the authorisation to transmit it to come through.

With cordial greetings,

Yours,

Freud

Berggasse 19,
Vienna IX,
13.4.1919

Dear Dr Pfister,

Before answering your informative letter of March 23 I waited for Rank to return, and also until I had found out about the effect of the events in Hungary. Now I am delighted to inform you that I too regard the foundation of the Zürich society as a very hopeful event, provided that the gentlemen, who are to a large extent novices, show themselves ready to work hard and do not waste their energy theorising and taking sides before being qualified to do so by experience. I am also of the opinion that the quality of the membership is more important than its quantity, and therefore appeal to you to put a tight rein on your kindliness, which makes you want to unite all conflicting elements; otherwise it will all end up again in a Jungian parody.

The psycho-analytic endowment which I administer is not an end in itself, but is available to be spent on worth-while objectives. Contributions will therefore gladly be made to the expenses for psycho-analytic purposes with which your group will be faced. But not for the time being, so long as our crown is worth only eighteen centimes and we have no credits at our disposal abroad. In these circumstances it would be wasting our substance to no purpose. For the same reason, Rank tells me, the publishing house will exercise reserve towards the Berne publishers.

It is also our firm intention that Dr Sachs shall stay in Switzerland permanently as a go-between, so that we may be guided by his judgment. Perhaps he may be useful to you as an itinerant instructor; he is an excellent speaker, and has the whole subject at his command.

According to all our information, the Soviet government in Hungary is well disposed rather than the reverse towards analysis, but the funds are not yet in our hands, and communications with Hungary are very difficult. Fortunately we have enough to go on with.

I do not see ordinary perverts, because they are not severely ill when they seek analysis from me.

With cordial greetings and best wishes,

Yours,

Freud

Berggasse 19,
Vienna IX,
27.5.1919

Dear Dr Pfister,

What a disagreeable task you have passed on to me.[1] The simplest thing to do in the case of men who are friends and both aspire to complete integrity and truth by way of psycho-analysis would be to send each the other's letter and let both discover for themselves where they are arguing at cross-purposes. However, I have never tried to evade an unpleasant task. I shall say to both of you what I have to criticise in both and to neither what I find fault with in the other.

First, your factual question, which can be answered with confidence. You have applied for admission to the International Psycho-Analytical Association and must regard your application as having been provisionally accepted. The lack of any reply from headquarters is explained by the

---

[1] There had been a disagreement between Pfister and Sachs

chance of its isolation because of the interruption of the postal service. You will see in the next number of the journal, which has already been printed, and is on the way here from Teschen, that your group's application has been acknowledged by headquarters.

That being the position, it is obvious that until the next congress no-one has any authority to turn you out. If Sachs advised you to withdraw, he did so purely in his private capacity, and you are not under the slightest obligation to follow his advice, as you could have told him quietly and with a good conscience, secure in the knowledge that your scientific beliefs qualify you for membership.

On the other hand, no-one has the power and no-one will try to keep you in the international association if you have no desire to remain in it. There is a good deal in your letter that points in that direction, but, if that is the situation, there seems to me to be no urgent reason why you should decide to withdraw immediately. Until the congress takes place (which will probably not be till 1920), you can wait and see whether the alleged antagonisms increase or decline, and whether or not you are able to get on with the members of the international association, and thus avoid all the harm that you fear might ensue for your society.

However, you want from me, not only the facts of the situation, but if possible also my backing. That I should gladly give you if I did not have something to reproach you with (and I mean in the first place you, Dr O. Pf., and not the Zürich association). In your letter there is not a syllable about what is the chief point of Sachs's letter. From the discussion, the reaction to the casual remarks he made, the ensuing argument with you, and probably also from all sorts of imponderabilia not communicable in writing, he received the impression that there existed in the society the intention to leave the factor of sexuality if possible untouched. I hope he was wrong in this conclusion, because when the society joined us it could not help knowing that this was its shibboleth. But perhaps he mistrusts 'Swiss

69

psychology' and fears that 'Jungification' has left a deeper mark on you than you are willing to admit to yourselves and others. Thus I should gladly say he was wrong if–the little word in question had occurred just once in your letter. That would have cleared up and facilitated so much. As it is, the impression is created of a symptomatic action confirming Sachs's suspicion.

Also I cannot believe that Sachs's unwarranted advice was based on the view that your society was not ready for association with the international association on the ground that the latter consisted of fully-fledged analysts. There must be a misunderstanding here. Sachs knows that (1) this is not true of the international association, and (2) that a new society cannot consist of fully-fledged analysts.

The other thing I dislike is the antagonism which, your letter testifies, has developed towards our friend Sachs. If the members of the society are so ready to regard him as an emissary of the High Inquisition sent to keep a watchful eye on their orthodoxy, that is a political reaction most inappropriate in a scientific context; the spirit of republican independence might with equal propriety rebel against the tyranny of the logarithm tables. A scientific society would be better advised to consider whether there was not much to be learnt from the advice and arguments of a tried and experienced man. I admit that but for this aspect of the matter I should not take the whole thing very seriously.

You should have taken Sachs's so fully forgetting his own advantage in what he said as a testimonial to his integrity and his disinclination to any kind of opportunism.

With this I conclude my judgment in the official role imposed upon me. Allow me in my private capacity to express the hope that you and Sachs will survive this 'storm' and derive from the experience a strengthened sense of what you hold in common.

With cordial greetings,

Yours,

Freud

Dear Dr Pfister,

In the process of clearing my desk before going away (Villa Wassing, Bad Gastein) your unanswered letter reminds me of my obligations. It arrived at a time of acute worry, particularly about our friends in Budapest, and writing was very much against the grain.

I received your Geneva news with great interest. There is much that is hopeful, but not yet any centre-point round which crystallisation can take place. I am delighted to endorse your liking for Mlle. Malan.[1] If you will vouch for her style and understanding, I shall be glad to allow her to translate any of my works she likes, subject to her publisher's acquiring the translation rights from my publishers (Deuticke, Heller) before January 1, 1920; otherwise I shall withdraw the authorisation. My endowment can do nothing to help; we can send no money abroad as long as the crown is so low. I should welcome a decision.

To the best of my knowledge I have given no authorisation to M. Gillet of Grenoble.

I congratulate you on the success of your *Method*. You will be receiving the second edition of *Leonardo* through the international psycho-analytical publishing house (Rank).

Dr Tausk[2] has committed suicide. He was a highly gifted man, but was a victim of fate, a delayed victim of the war. Did you know him?

I am very pleased that you and Sachs are again on good terms. But does the society take any part in his courses, etc.?

According to your reports it would be really desirable to bring the wild analysis in Switzerland under control.

With cordial greetings,

Yours,

Freud

[1] H. Malan, Pfister's French translator
[2] Dr Viktor Tausk, Vienna psycho-analyst

POSTCARD   *Badersee, near Garmisch,*
                                        31.8.1919
Dear Dr Pfister,

Thank you for your recent letters, which have remained
unanswered in the commotion of travel, and for sending me
Mordell's book,[1] which I am reading with great interest. I
have been having a quiet rest here, and shall not be returning
to our gloomy conditions until the last week in September.

                                      Cordially yours,
                                            Freud

                                      Berggasse 19,
                                       Vienna IX,
                                       5.10.1919
Dear Dr Pfister,

I have to thank you for a number of letters of recent
months which in the upheaval of absence on holiday I did
not always answer. I have been back since September 24, and
shall now again become a reliable correspondent. I have been
hearing a great deal of pleasing news about you and your
work from Rank and Jones. Jones left yesterday.

Ferenczi has at last got away from Budapest, and is now
here. He has handed over the presidency, the duties of which
he cannot discharge in these times, to Jones (until the next
congress). Official arrangements are in hand.

My son Martin, having returned home from his Italian
imprisonment, has now surrendered to another; he has
become engaged to the girl of his choice, a Vienna lawyer's
daughter.

In regard to your friendly proposition regarding the French
translation of the *Interpretation of Dreams* or the *Introductory
Lectures*, the reply must be that I am reserving these tasks for
our international publishing house, which is now preparing
for the publication of a British journal under Jones's editor-
ship, but is only awaiting the opportunity of bringing out

[1] Albert Mordell, *The Erotic Motive in Literature*, London, 1919

works in French. Bircher's negotiations with our publishing house have not led to anything, so far as I know, and therefore I cannot take him into consideration.

With cordial greetings,
Yours,
Freud

Berggasse 19,
Vienna IX,
27.12.1919

Dear Dr Pfister,

Your first utterance since leaving here again betrays the active philanthropist. I have no authority to thank you, but I can say that it is very fine. Because of the holidays I cannot pass on the matter to Wagner[1] till tomorrow. What do you say to an administration that shrieks to the outside world for aid and then does not admit it when it comes?

Your son, provided that he has inherited anything at all from his father, will be very welcome. Rank, with all his treasures and novelties, is expected here on the thirtieth. Then we shall set about getting your book ready for the press; Hitschmann's *Gottfried Keller* is already out.

We shall have an abundance of articles from which to select for the next few numbers of the journal and *Imago*. Among them is a particularly interesting paper by Muralt[2] which, in spite of certain difficulties, we do not want to leave out. What do you think he would say to a detailed criticism of his paper? If he is willing to accept this, and has retained a copy with similarly numbered pages, I should like to try it. He is in the best possible state of defection from Jung, but he obviously read Jung and Jung only before reading me, with the result that he ascribes to him a great deal

[1] Professor Julius von Wagner-Jauregg (1857–1940), who had been asked by the Zürich Society for Aiding the Mentally Sick to undertake the responsibility jointly with Freud of distributing food parcels to mentally sick persons in Vienna

[2] Presumably *Ein Pseudoprophet*, a psycho-analytical study by Alexander von Muralt, Munich, 1920

of which he is as guiltless as he is of spectral analysis, while with a very few exceptions he objects to everything that is really his. Also I should like to eliminate a few personal remarks, such as his comparison of Jung's style with mine, and Jung's private statement that he does not reject me, and graciously allows me my place, but merely corrects me and makes me 'fit for polite society'.[1] I should like to win over rather than put off the worthy but still obviously very inexperienced Muralt.

My daughter will gladly continue the collection for you which my son began. I hope you will be coming with a children's train again. Let us alter the saying and say: Suffer me to come with the little children.

Let us see whether 1920 can make good much of what the five previous years have spoilt. In any case, may it bring nothing but good to you.

Cordially yours,

Freud

Berggasse 19,
Vienna IX,
27.1.1920

Dear Dr Pfister,

You sent us a charming lad, who, moreover, introduced himself with the traditional gifts. On the telephone his voice sounded so much like yours that for a while I could not believe it belonged to the second generation; and at lunch on Sunday he did not seem in the least unfamiliar; and he behaved so naturally that it was a delight to have him.

In spite of that, since Sunday we have not seen him again. On the same afternoon we received the news that our dear Sophie in Hamburg had been snatched away by influenzal pneumonia, snatched away from glowing health, from her busy life as a capable mother and loving wife, in four or five days, as if she had never been. We had been worried about

---

[1] *Zimmerrein,* more literally 'house-trained'

74

her for two days, but were still hopeful. From a distance it is so difficult to judge. The distance still remains. We could not, as we wished to, go to her at once when the first alarming news came, because there were no trains, not even a children's train.[1] The undisguised brutality of our time weighs heavily on us. Our poor Sunday child is to be cremated to-morrow. Not till the day after to-morrow will our daughter Mathilde and her husband, thanks to an unexpected concatenation of circumstances, be able to set off for Hamburg in an Entente train. At least our son-in-law was not alone. Two of our sons who were in Berlin are already with him, and our friend Eitingon[2] has gone with them.

Sophie leaves behind two boys, one aged six and the other thirteen months, and an inconsolable husband who will have to pay dearly for the happiness of these seven years. The happiness was only between them, not in external circumstances, which were war and war service, being wounded and losing their money, but they remained brave and cheerful.

I do as much work as I can, and am grateful for the distraction. The loss of a child seems to be a grave blow to one's narcissism; as for mourning, that will no doubt come later.

However, as soon as the condolences have been coped with, Pfister junior shall come and see us. It is not the lad's fault, after all. He has already sent us a card of sympathy.

Feeling sure of your sympathy and with cordial greetings,

Yours,

Freud

P.S. Please thank Oberholzer[3] for me, and ask him to excuse me because of this painful experience.

[1] Children from starving Austria were sent abroad by an international children's aid association
[2] Dr Max Eitingon (1881–1943), founder of the Berlin Psycho-Analytic Clinic and the Palestinian Psycho-Analytical Society
[3] Dr Emil Oberholzer, Swiss psycho-analyst

Zürich,
11.3.1920
Dear Professor Freud,

That you should have done me the honour of correcting my work[1] with your own hand is very kind of you. I have carefully checked your criticisms and suggested amendments, and found them all justified. The work will certainly benefit greatly by your sponsorship. I have corrected the proofs in accordance with my conscience, and, I am sure, your judgment. The only thing I cannot pack into my rucksack is your joke about philosophy. If my philosophy amuses you . . . we are quits, and you come off the better. . . .

Berggasse 19,
Vienna IX,
9.5.1920
Dear Dr Pfister,

Your polypragmasia fills me with admiration, and I am delighted at the progress your book is making with us. You have been in Florence and Rome, and I have been very envious of you, in spite of the bugs.

General rules about when analysis should be declined are hard to give at present. It would be a subject for discussion at a meeting at which experiences could be exchanged.

I very much liked your St Paul,[2] which seems to me to be better fitted for *Imago*, of which it will be an ornament, than for your book, which is swelling as it is. I have always had a special sympathy for St Paul as a genuinely Jewish character. Is he not the only one who stands completely in the light of history?

Yesterday, as a member of the committee, I attended the opening of the children's home called the Tivoli. It is a

---

[1] Presumably O. Pfister, *Zum Kampf um die Psychoanalyse*, Internationale Psychoanalytische Verlag, 1920. Psychoanalytische Schriften. 1921. (*Some Applications of Psycho-Analysis*, Allen and Unwin, London, 1923)

[2] O. Pfister, *Die Entwicklung des Apostel Paulus. Eine religionsgeschichtliche und psychologische Skizze.* Imago, 1920

German American endowment to which my New York brother-in-law[1] contributed a million crowns. Vienna is really becoming more and more impossible. But the hospitality of the Limmat valley, at any rate the official variety, is also uninviting.

With cordial greetings from
Your continually ageing
Freud

Berggasse 19,
Vienna IX,
21.6.1920

Dear Dr Pfister,

I picked up your little book[2] on expressionism with as much interest as aversion, and read it through at a sitting. Then I found I liked it very much, not so much the purely analytical part, which cannot overcome the difficulty of communication to non-analysts, but the links you establish with the subject and what you make of them. It kept reminding me of what a good, kind person, you are. This Pfister, I said to myself, is a man to whom any kind of unfairness is totally alien, you cannot compare yourself to him, and how lucky it is that you cannot help agreeing with everything that he comes across in his path. For you must know that in practice I am dreadfully intolerant of fools, see only the harmful side of them, and that, so far as these 'artists' are concerned, I am actually one of those whom you brand at the outset as philistines and barbarians. You explain clearly and exhaustively why these people lack the right to claim the name of artist.

Please accept my warm thanks for this enrichment of my psycho-analytical treasure.

Your devoted
Freud

P.S. What is your charming son doing?

[1] Ely Bernays, Freud's wife's brother, was married to Freud's sister Anna

[2] *Der psychologische und biologische Untergrund expressionistischer Bilder,* Berne, 1920. (*Expressionism in Art, Its Psychological and Biological Basis,* Kegan Paul, London, 1922; New York, 1923)

77

...I have now spoken in public about psycho-analysis four times in succession in various places, and each time with great outward success. The teachers of a large part of the canton of Zürich have placed themselves solidly behind me, and are calling on the highest authorities to give teachers the opportunity of becoming acquainted with pedagogic psycho-analysis (paedanalysis). . . .

POSTCARD   *Vienna,*
                                    28.11.1920
Dear Dr Pfister,
    Almost simultaneously with the first copy of your book, on which I congratulate you, there arrived your tribute to Flournoy,[1] which I liked so much that I should like you to write something similar about him for our journal, emphasising his connection with psycho-analysis.[2] I think Flournoy has a claim to such an appreciation, and I do not think anyone will challenge you on that.
    How is your son? Still in Paris?

                            Cordially yours,
                                        Freud

                            Berggasse 19,
                            Vienna IX,
                            25.12.1920
Dear Dr Pfister,
    Your two Bircher books[3] and your letter have just dropped in through the letter-box for Christmas. I have skimmed

---

[1] Pfister's obituary of Theodore Flournoy, Swiss mystic, in the *Neue Zürcher Zeitung,* 1920
[2] Pfister's tribute appeared in the *Internationale Zeitschrift fur Psychoanalyse,* 1921–7, pp. 101–6
[3] (1) See footnote 2, p. 77; (2) O. Pfister, *Die Behandlung schwer erziehbarer und abnormer Kinder*

through the two former and confess that they are very good, much better than I expected. They will provide a useful means of propaganda and education. I see that a volume by Silberer on the imp of the unconscious is announced,[1] and I am curious to see how the fox will come to terms with psycho-analysis in the matter and how he will drag in his anagogics.

A few days ago I received the number of the *Revue de Genève* containing the first lecture of the *Psycho-analysis*,[2] and a few days before that I received a Danish translation of it. It is true that things are moving everywhere, but you seem to over-estimate my pleasure in that. What personal pleasure is to be derived from analysis I obtained during the time when I was alone, and since others have joined me it has given me more pain than pleasure. The way people accept and distort it has not changed the opinion I formed of them when they non-understandingly rejected it. An incurable breach must have come into existence at that time between me and other men.

I watched your small battle with Rank from a distance, and of course was entirely on his side. You were wrong when you tried to pin him down to what he said at your inaugural meeting. All the circumstances have completely changed since then. Our crown, if I am not very much mistaken, still stood at between four and five centimes, and since then the expenses of the publishing house have certainly quintupled. It was therefore very unreasonable and unco-operative of the Swiss to ask for preferential treatment affecting our very possibility of existence instead of taking into consideration the difficult position of the publishing house. Every consideration would have been shown to an individual who confessed his poverty, which would certainly be nothing to be ashamed of, least of all to beggars like us. I was unable to understand what Swiss national pride was aiming at in the matter; all it could do was exploit the dreadful weakness of our currency.

[1] Herbert Silberer, *Der Zufall and die Koboldstreiche des Unbewussten*, Bircher, Berne, 1921
[2] The first French translation of the *Five Lectures*. See footnote 1, p. 37

I am glad to hear that you have withdrawn your objection.

I am delighted that the proposal to produce a jubilee volume in my honour has gone overboard. I am extraordinarily opposed to celebrations. But we hope to fish up and bring ashore the paper you intended to write for it. With cordial greetings and best wishes for Christmas and the New Year.

Your devoted
Freud

PFISTER TO FREUD   *14.1.1921*

... I have made a wonderful discovery in Plato which will give you pleasure. Nachmansohn in his paper[1] missed the most important thing of all. Plato wrote the following: 'For the art of healing . . . is knowledge of the body's loves . . . and he who is able to distinguish between the good and bad kinds, and is able to bring about a change, so that the body acquires one kind of love instead of the other, and is able to impart love to those in whom there is none . . . is the best physician.' Plato traces back all art, religion, morality, to love, and he also has an admirable knowledge of the unconscious, the conflicting aspirations of the mind. . . .

POSTCARD   *Vienna,*
                                                       4.2.1921
Dear Dr Pfister,
     I am very glad you have had things out in such a friendly way with Rank. I hope it leaves no trace behind. Your little paper on Plato[2] is very welcome, *celà va sans dire*. I energetically defend Groddeck[3] against your respectability. What

---

[1] Max Nachmansohn, *Freuds Libidotheorie verglichen mit der Lehre Platos*, *Zeitschrift*, 1915, No. 3, pp. 63–83
[2] O. Pfister, *Plato als Vorläufer der Psychoanalyse*. *Zentralblatt*, 1921
[3] Dr Georg Walther Groddeck (1866–1934), German psycho-analyst and writer

PFISTER TO FREUD   *Zürich,*
                                         14.3.1921
. . . I understand very well that it is impossible for you to
think otherwise. The state of mind that leads you to en-
courage Groddeck is exactly the same as that which made
you the discoverer and pioneer of psycho-analysis. But, with
the best will in the world, I cannot adopt your view, as
indeed you do not expect me to. But there is a big difference
between Rabelais and Groddeck. The former remains within
his role as a satirist and avoids the error of putting himself
forward as a savant. Groddeck, however, wavers between
science and belles lettres. You say yourself that his trend is
definitely scientific, but I dislike his spicing it with jokes. I
like a clean sheet of paper, and I also like fresh butter, but
butter-stains on a sheet of paper satisfy neither my eye nor
my belly. His interpretations are too Stekelian for me. . . .

                                         Berggasse 19,
                                         Vienna IX,
                                         23.3.1921
Dear Dr Pfister,
    I should of course be glad to accept a woman doctor for
self-analysis,[1] provided that she is prepared to pay the now
usual forty francs an hour and remains long enough for there
to be a prospect of getting somewhere, *i.e.,* from four to six
months; a shorter period is not worth while. I could certainly
take her on October 1; whether I could take her earlier it is

[1] *I.e.,* training analysis

impossible to say. I am waiting to hear whether two patients due to begin on April 1 are really coming.

You do not mention in your letter how much time the young woman is willing to devote to analysis. How her recent marriage will accord with an analysis lasting for many months I cannot say, so further information is desirable.

I was delighted with your remarks about Groddeck. We really must be able to tell each other home-truths, *i.e.*, incivilities, and remain firm friends, as in this case. I am not giving up my view of Groddeck either, I am usually not so easily taken in by anybody. But it does not matter.

What you say about the pleasure principle is interesting and valuable. You will soon have occasion to express your opinion on a new piece, *Group Psychology and the Analysis of the Ego*. On the other hand, what you say about dreaming seems to me to be only classificatory in nature. Let us not forget the broadest and best definition of dreaming, which is that it is the mental activity that takes place during sleep.

With cordial greetings to you and, please, also to the Oberholzers.

Yours,
Freud

POSTCARD   *Vienna,*
                                                     17.4.1921
Dear Dr Pfister,

How dare you meddle in things that have nothing to do with you? What business have you being ill?

Your paper[1] will certainly rouse interest in *Imago*, but decide for yourself where it will be the more effective from your point of view. Whatever you decide will be acceptable to us.

Cordially yours,
Freud

[1] *Experimental Dreams concerning Theoretical Subjects, Psyche and Eros,* 1921

Berggasse 19,
Vienna IX,
20.5.1921

Dear Dr Pfister,

It is of course a disgrace that I have not long since answered your cordial telegram of May 6. In self-defence I must plead a deceptive memory; until to-day's big raid on my desk I really believed I had done so long ago. Thus all I can do is belatedly express my satisfaction that a holy man like you has not allowed himself to be scared of such a heretical relationship. May it continue to bring happiness both to you and us, as in the past.

Actually, of course, you have long since been accepted into the family.

In the expectation that you will remain devoted to it ('much prized and much rebuked'), I remain, perhaps for some years yet,

Your devoted
Freud

Berggasse 19,
Vienna IX,
3.11.1921

Dear Dr Pfister,

I always read your letters with pleasure, they are always so full of life, warmth and success. So let me congratulate you on your latest achievements and hope that your publisher's difficulties will be temporary.

Fräulein E. is not with me, but with Rank, who praises her highly. I could not take her, as British and American doctors have been taking up all my time. So I now work for dollars and cannot manage anything else.

Otherwise there is little to report. The family, who send you their very great thanks, are well. In the past six months their numbers have been increased by two small boys, one in

Vienna and the other in Berlin. A great-grandmother of eighty-six still survives.

Your criticism of the 'Pulveriser'[1] is very dignified.

With cordial greetings,

Yours,

Freud

PFISTER TO FREUD

Zürich,

3.4.1922

Dear Professor Freud,

I had hoped to give you a little pleasure by sending you a new book, but now the pleasure is overshadowed by a great sorrow. Yesterday we lost our ablest analyst, Dr Rorschach.[2] He died of peritonitis, and leaves a widow (herself a qualified physician) and two children completely without resources. He had a wonderfully clear and original mind, was devoted to analysis heart and soul, and threw in his lot with you down to the smallest details. His 'diagnostic test', which would perhaps better be called analysis of form, was admirably worked out. During the last three weeks I sent him three series of tests done with his blots, giving him only the age and sex of the individual concerned, and his diagnoses were excellent, though the cases were extremely complicated. One patient is a young girl who for years has been continually weeping and wanting to die and is totally incapable of work. From the tests Rorschach immediately diagnosed an obsessional neurosis with sadistic and confabulatory trends. This, as well as many other features of the case which he detected, was fully corroborated. He addressed the psycho-analytical society only a few weeks ago on the application of his methods to psycho-analysis (I hope his lecture will be printed). His intention was to become a university teacher. He was a poor man all his life, and a proud, upright man of great human kindness, and he is a great loss to us.

[1] O. Pfister, *Einstampfen! Eine Richtigstellung in Sachen der Psycho-analyse, Schulreform,* 1921

[2] Dr Hermann Rorschach (1884–1922), Swiss psychiatrist and neurologist

84

Professor Schneider recently wrote to me from Riga about the great successes he was having with Rorschach's tests. Can you not do something to verify his really magnificent testing system, which is certain to be of great service to psychoanalysis? I am glad that I was able at the time to persuade Bircher to print Rorschach's pioneering work. His widow's address is Irrenanstalt Herisau, Canton of Appenzell.

I am taking the liberty of making just one short observation about the book[1] I am sending you to-day. It represents an advance, in so far as I have finally overcome a great many confusions to which I had succumbed because of Jung and Adler. So, to my great pleasure, I can say without doubt or reservation that I have now seen the correctness of your views even in areas where for a long time I had no experience of my own. In matters of ethics, religion, and philosophy there remain differences between us which neither you nor I regard as a gulf. In my new work, which is the first volume of a monograph on the development and aberrations of love, I address myself to parents and teachers, because my faith in the pundits has notably shrunk. My primary aim is to help to overcome distress, and this is better done by pointing out to people the way to the psycho-analyst than by battling with the serried ranks of thick-headed psychologists and educationists. But it is incredibly difficult to write simply and at the same time cover the ground thoroughly. I took a great deal of trouble to combine the two objectives in this book, I do not know if I have succeeded. . . .

Berggasse 19,
Vienna IX,
6.4.1922

Dear Dr Pfister,

Thank you for your latest book, which arrived to-day, after your letter. All I know of it so far is from opening the

---

[1] O. Pfister, *Die Liebe des Kindes und ihre Fehlentwicklungen,* Bircher, Berne, 1922 (*Love in Children and its Aberrations,* Allen and Unwin, London, 1924)

parcel, but I suspect that it will be my favourite among the creatures of your mind and, in spite of Jesus Christ and occasional obeisances to anagogics, the closest to my own way of thinking. Complete objectivity requires a person who takes less pleasure in life than you do; you insist on finding something edifying in it. True, it is only in old age that one is converted to the grim heavenly pair λόγος καὶ ἀνάγκη.

Rorschach's death is very sad. I shall write a few words to his widow to-day. My impression is that perhaps you overrate him as an analyst; I note with pleasure from your letter the high esteem in which you hold him as a man. Of course no-one but you shall write the tribute to him in the journal, and please write it soon.

Your admirable rebuff to Lipps[1] serves him right. I think you have summed up Häberlin admirably.[2] In the matter of H. it is hard to know what to advise. It often happens that excellent and serious men cannot help hurting each other, because otherwise they cannot give full expression to their love. It is not to be taken too seriously.

When we talk about you, we always think of your astonishing capacity for and pleasure in work, the very things for which with less justification you praise me.

With cordial greetings and thanks,

Yours,
Freud

PFISTER TO FREUD   *Zürich,*
                                  19.7.1922

. . . As for the anagogics you think you can detect in my other potboiler, I am completely innocent of the charge. What matter to analysis are catagogics. I have completely finished with the Jungian manner. Those high-falutin inter-

---

[1] Gottlieb Friedrich Lipps (1865–1931), psychologist and philosopher, Professor in Leipzig University, later of Zurich

[2] O. Pfister, *Zwei Erziehungsbücher von Professor Paul Häberlin, Religiöess Volksblatt,* 1922. Paul Haberlin (1878–1959), Swiss psychologist and educationist, was a professor in Berne and later in Zurich

pretations which proclaim every kind of muck to be spiritual jam of a high order and try to smuggle a minor Apollo or Christ into every corked-up little mind simply will not do. It is Hegelianism transferred to psychology; everything that is must be reasonable. If only that theory were true!

But education is quite different, it definitely must have an ethical meaning. You yourself used to insist that children have to be educated. And, when analysis is over and done with, the little beasts and angels with whom we have to deal have to be filled with honourable intentions. Not that one should blow upon them with the breath of the spirit and blow one's soul into them; but they must have a bit of mental and social hygiene and practise it with healthy love. But analysis as such must take all witch's brews seriously, adorn the devil with no fig leaves, and do full justice to the parable of the tares among the wheat. . .

Bad Gastein,
25.7.1922

Dear Dr Pfister,

At last a letter with which I am in heartfelt agreement— with the exception of one point. This concerns your sudden inclination to (ordinary and medically induced) self-damage. Is this punishment for your conversion from anagogics to catagogics?

Of course there must be education, and it can even be strict; it does it no harm if it is based on analytic knowledge, but analysis itself is after all something quite different and is in the first place an honest establishment of the facts, in that we are in agreement. A squeamish concern that no harm must be done to the higher things in man is unworthy of an analyst.

I am glad you are satisfied with your colleague; we are finding that not easy. We cannot get anything out of him. When at last he promises a contribution to the journal, it never turns up, and when he undertakes to write a tribute to a valued colleague who has died, no tribute comes. Though he is president of a local group, he never appears at congresses, and no doubt will not do so at the next, and that is really unprecedented.

Certainly I shall find time to talk to you and Binswanger about poor Frau H. But will it do her any good? The unwise creature has lost her lawsuit with life, I think in the court of every instance. At the time I made the most uncommon efforts to avert the verdict.

I too am greatly looking forward to our meeting again. For a long time I have felt no desire to lecture. I know I shall be pressed to do so.

Now devote yourself energetically to getting completely well again.

With cordial greetings,

Yours,

Freud

My address from the beginning of August will be Gebirgskurhaus am Obersalzberg.

Berggasse 19,

Vienna IX,

Christmas 1922

Dear Dr Pfister,

At last a few free days in which to catch up with arrears of correspondence. Normally I am a conscientious correspondent, but during the past weeks I have dropped behind. I have now reduced my working day to seven hours, and promised myself that never again will it be nine.

Your complete and ever more manifest defection from Jung and Adler has given me great satisfaction for a long time past. Now I can definitely advise you not to reject your meritorious book,[1] which has already acquired such a good reputation in the world, but to revise it, and thus let it keep pace with your own development. You should do the same

---

[1] O. Pfister, *Die psychoanalytische Methode*, see footnote 4, p. 55

with other works of yours in so far as the same situation applies.

Your new book or booklet will also be welcome after Christmas; its arrival will be acknowledged by postcard. For your collection apply direct to those of our members who seem desirable to you as authors and suggest the subject yourself. I shall try to get the publishing house to accept the posy.

In general we are passing through difficult times here, the effects of which on the publishing house I am trying to fend off. News of the immediate family is good. Ernst in Berlin has got himself a second son. I now have the younger of my Hamburg grandsons here with my eldest, childless daughter. In the wider family there are always worries, of course.

With cordial greeting to you and yours and best wishes far into 1923.

Yours,
Freud

POSTCARD   *Vienna,*
                                                19.3.1923
Dear Dr Pfister,

I have since heard that you have acquired pains in the knee on the occasion of your half-century celebrations and I send you my heartiest congratulations, on the latter at any rate, on an open postcard so that everyone can read it and join in.

Good luck to you!

Yours,
Freud

PFISTER TO FREUD   *23.10.1923*

Dear Professor Freud,

I can give you the welcome news that all is in order again in our Swiss society. . . .

89

When things get serious everyone realises what a great and magnificent thing analysis is, and what an enrichment of life it means to him. It brought an unparalleled illumination into my life, and I cannot thank you enough for all you have done for me by your discoveries and your personal kindness to me. If I am able to work really hard for analysis during the years that remain to me I shall be a happy man, no matter what other things life may have in store for me. Also I rejoice that the small band that met at Weimar in 1911 has grown into a whole army that looks up to you in admiration and venëration. Now care must be taken to ensure that the wine of your work is not watered down. I am delighted that Berlin now insists on a three-year training course in psycho-analysis. If anything, that is on the short side. . . .

Seventeen volumes either written or edited by me now stand on my book-shelf, including translations. Should I not slow down a bit? But it is so hard not to write when one has learnt such great and important things from you. . . .

POSTCARD   *Vienna,*
                                          30.10.1923
Dear Dr Pfister,
    Do not allow yourself to be put off by the number seventeen, but go on working. You know that the truth often has to be said many times.
    I am temporarily out of action as a consequence of my latest operation, but I shall be back in the ranks again in a few weeks.

                                    Cordially yours,
                                            Freud

PFISTER TO FREUD   *Zürich,*
                                          30.12.1923
    . . . It is now nearly fifteen years since I entered your house for the first time and quickly fell in love with your humani-

90

tarian character and the free and cheerful spirit of your whole family. The little girl who took care of the lizards, who now writes very serious papers for the International Psycho-Analytical Association, was still in short skirts, and your second son played truant from school in order to introduce the boring frock-coated old pastor to the mysteries of the Prater. In the box with you, your charming wife and your witty sister-in-law, I felt as if I were in a divine, Olympian abode, and if I had been asked what was the most agreeable place in the world I could only have replied: 'Find out at Professor Freud's'. . . .

Berggasse 19,
Vienna IX,
4.1.1924

Dear Dr Pfister,

Your cordial New Year's letter celebrating the fifteen-year jubilee of our friendship gave me great pleasure. You have the gift of throwing a rosy sheen over the everyday life one takes part in so colourlessly. I also thank you for saying so little about my illness, which during the past few months has been taking up much too much space in our lives.

You ask whether I can take Herr P. for analysis during the summer. It is hard for me to undertake any commitments for the summer, because I am not yet quite certain about the future. But, if I can, I shall certainly do so, provided that he comes of his own accord. Also do not forget that I do not work during the real summer months.

We had the impression here that your society had rather gone to sleep, as we heard that no meeting had been held for months, so I am glad to hear that you have woken up. Things are lively here too; let me refer you to the latest productions of our publishing house.

With hearty best wishes for 1924,

Yours,

Freud

Zürich,
14.2.1924
. . . The book by Ferenczi and Rank[1] has given me a lot of hard nuts to crack. That psycho-analysis is leading to a new outlook on life I cannot and will not admit. All analysis can do is make valuable contributions to building up such an outlook. The latter depends on synthesis, and one must beware of overloading the psycho-analytical apple-cart. You yourself have always taught that what matters is not remembering but reliving, in that you have always insisted that memory is not sufficient, but that it must be charged with affect. It is exaggerated to say that after the ideal treatment one would never hear of the patient again. It is only human that gratitude, even if not effusive gratitude, should remain; that does not involve any sacrifice of liberty. . . .

Berggasse 19,
Vienna IX,
26.2.1924
Dear Dr Pfister,
Your book has once more given me pleasure in its splendid English guise.[2] You should be satisfied with the impact that your efforts are having.

I have also received a pile of publications from Beltrano in Buenos Aires. You are no longer *up to date*[3] in contrasting my world renown with the indifference of Vienna. This month the *Neue Presse* actually published an article about my humble person, and there is a book in the bookshops by a pupil of Stekel's which is written in a not too unfriendly manner and tries to assess 'the man, his work, and his school'.[4]

[1] S. Ferenczi and O. Rank, *Entwicklungsziele der Psychoanalyse*, Vienna, 1924
[2] O. Pfister, *Love in Children and its Aberrations*, Allen & Unwin, London, 1924
[3] These three words in English in the original
[4] Dr Fritz Wittels (1880–1950), *Sigmund Freud, der Mann, die Lehre, die Schule*, Leipzig, 1924

The new work of Ferenczi and Rank is having a very stimulating and rather exciting effect in our circles too. I hope discussions of the matter will lead to some progress.

You are the only one of my friends who does not mention my illness in your letters, but I assume you will be glad to hear that I am getting on with my work and expect further improvement from the treatment, which is not yet over.

With cordial greetings,
Yours,
Freud

PFISTER TO FREUD *Zürich*,
29.4.1924

. . . The congress[1] gave me a great deal. You were present in a much more real sense than at earlier congresses, at which the negative father transference kept peeping through. We were all of course tremendously pleased to see you there in person, and quite a number came especially in that hope. But everyone gladly granted you your well-deserved rest on the Semmering. Many of the papers gave me great pleasure. One or two things struck me as being too ambitious for a lecture, particularly the metapsychological. A danger that is still very noticeable is that of false generalisation; your pupils rush in where you weigh things up carefully. Jones traced back many character traits to the small intestine, Abraham favoured the beginning of the digestive tract, and Simmel either the middle or the whole end part of it. In this process someone ascribed a number of character traits to an organ to which someone else attributed entirely different traits. So far as I am concerned, someone can come along and describe the belly or the oesophagus as an element in character formation, and he can be followed by someone else who takes some other organ to be found in the neighbourhood of the alimentary canal, some gland or other, or the pituitary

[1] Eighth congress of the International Psycho-Analytical Association at Salzburg

gland, or what you will. In the long run people will see that it does not do to stake everything on one card, but that conditions must be considered as a whole. Also the extent to which organic functions are psychologically determined must be examined, otherwise one may relapse into the cold and rather skinny arms of Adler. . . .

Berggasse 19,
Vienna IX,
11.5.1924

Dear Dr Pfister,

Thank you for your account of the congress and your good wishes for my birthday.

As usual, of course, you are hard at your labours, the fruits of which always give me pleasure. I think that the publishing house will gladly accept and publish the posthumous works of Rorschach. That will of course depend on their length and content. I should like to postpone a decision in the matter, because Rank is in New York, and I do not wish to decide in his absence. However, you do not seem to have finished editing them yet.

It amused me greatly that you objected both to the organic foundations and the metapsychological superstructure. In reality, of course, one has to work at all levels at the same time.

You certainly have my permission to use any picture you like of me. If you do not like any of those that you have available, I shall send you the publishing house's latest full-face photograph. Whether a picture will show the 'good man' you insist on introducing to the public is of course something I cannot say.

With cordial greetings,
Yours,
Freud

Berggasse 19,
Vienna IX,
9.6.1924
Dear Dr Pfister,

Your *Psycho-Analytic Method*, which is still your most important book, has reached me, and after its transformation has still more claim for praise and good wishes for its success. I hope you will not take amiss two small observations. The first is that you are guilty of an inaccuracy, in a supremely unimportant matter, it is true, in Note 1 on page 2, where you give personal details about me. Actually I was never a full professor of neurology and was never anything but a lecturer. I became a titular professor in 1902 and a titular full professor in 1920, have never given up my academic post, but have continued with it for thirty-two years, and finally gave up my voluntary lectures in 1918. All that is very unimportant, but perhaps a critic might seize on this minor inaccuracy to cast doubt on your accuracy in general.

My second observation is that you still show too much respect for the poverty of Adler. Just ask yourself what difference it would make to your work if you had never heard of the Adlerian theory.

The book must contain a whole mass of other mistakes but, as I share them with you, I cannot detect them or criticise you for them.

At the beginning of July we are proposing to go to Waldhaus Flims in Graubünden for six or seven weeks. Perhaps you will be able to pop over and see us.

With cordial greetings,

Yours,

Freud

Berggasse 19,
Vienna IX,
21.12.1924

Dear Dr Pfister,

What a truly delightful Christmas greeting. I have of course not yet read your new book,[1] but only sampled it when I unpacked the parcel. But I am already sure that it is a good, bold, intelligent piece of work. Your productivity is beginning to put mine to shame, and I have not been in the least lazy in my time. May all the good spirits in which you still seem to believe give you the strength and will to maintain it for several more decades.

I am very satisfied with the choice of Lucerne for the next congress, but it is very doubtful whether I shall be able to travel to Switzerland to attend it in September. Travelling is nowadays a very serious undertaking for me. Abraham,[2] optimist as he is, will have told you the facts of the matter.

Do not worry about your young American. The man can be helped. Dr Reik[3] here in Vienna has specialised in these severe obsessional neuroses; he treated a Russian count whom I sent him, for instance, with extreme patience and deep understanding, and not without success, for several years.

You will be getting an *Autobiographical Study* shortly; I am expecting it soon.

With hearty Christmas greetings and good wishes for the jubilee year 1925,

Cordially yours,

Freud

Zulliger's excellent little book arrived to-day.[4]

---

[1] Presumably O. Pfister, *Die Liebe vor der Ehe und ihre Fehlentwicklungen,* Bircher, Berne, 1924

[2] Dr Karl Abraham (1877–1925), founder of the German Psycho-Analytical Society

[3] Dr Theodor Reik, Vienna psycho-analyst, now in New York

[4] Hans Zulliger, *Psychoanalytische Erfahrungen aus der Volkschulpraxis,* Bircher, Berne, 1921

Berggasse 19,
Vienna IX,
22.2.1925

Dear Dr Pfister,

Your praise for my charitableness and wisdom may perhaps be not entirely justified. If I did not know what a strange man the colleague about whom you write is in other respects also, I should take very much amiss his conduct in the matter of the congress. But I tell myself, as you do, that the man is not to be changed, and must therefore be swallowed as he is.

The prospect of having you with us here in Vienna at Easter is, so to speak, a consolation. Bring your American with you. Since you make such a strong plea for him, I am not disinclined to accept him for treatment in November. It is not correct that as a matter of principle I take doctors only. I have two patients among my five analysands at present,[1] and shall be glad to have a third for next season. My uniform fee is $20 an hour. As nature seems to be intending to grant me one or perhaps several more years of honour, I no longer need to fend off patients so anxiously. The main thing will of course be the impression the young man makes on me when we meet. Until October you will have to keep him yourself, because I see absolutely no possibility of taking him sooner.

Easter is not far off, and until then I send you my heartiest greetings.

Yours,
Freud

Berggasse 19,
Vienna IX,
10.5.1925

Dear Dr Pfister,

You were one of the few who sent personal congratulations in spite of the distance. In return, after an incubation period

[1] *I.e.,* Freud was conducting three training analyses

of a few days, you will be getting a permanent place among the like-minded in my room.[1]

Meanwhile I have met your protégé's parents. They seem very willing to make sacrifices, which generally points to a bad prognosis. I could promise them nothing definite, but could only indicate my general willingness. Perhaps I may be able to take the lad on September 1 instead of October 1. It is my strong wish that he should remain with you until then. His father is, I think, very tractable, but his mother seems more restless and more ready to undertake plans of her own.

We shall probably have further dealings over him.

With cordial greetings,

Yours,

Freud

Villa Schüler,
Semmering,
10.8.1925

Dear Dr Pfister,

So you are back at work again. I have been up here for six weeks and still have not had enough of idling.

As for our young hopeful, I think you should let him go to his ruin. There is a vague possibility that I might be able to take him on September 15, or perhaps even on September 1, but the almost insuperable difficulty is that with his unsociability there is nothing whatever for him to do at Semmering, so that I should run the risk of excessively occupying myself with him. In Vienna that would be something which would take care of itself.

My daughter will give you my greetings at Homburg.[2]

Cordially yours,

Freud

[1] The reference is to a photograph of Pfister's
[2] The seventh psycho-analytic congress at Homburg

Zürich,
8.10.1925
. . . Your tendency to resignation distresses me. If I took
you literally, I should object that you had handed over to
your id full power over life and death, good fortune and ill
fortune; and, in the name of your charming daughter, your
delightful wife, your whole family, science, and the whole
pantheon of supreme powers, I should protest. Two years
ago, on the occasion of my fiftieth birthday, you wrote to me
humorously that I was paying for it with a stiff leg. From
that moment onwards the trouble rapidly receded – the mas-
scuse would claim that she had something to do with it.
More than ten years ago you wrote to me dolefully that you
feared the time when your powers would decline, and since
then you have demonstrated unprecedented productivity and
greatness. In these circumstances I am not sure whether it is
more wickedness or love that makes me unable at present to
work up a proper veneration for the age which you emphasise. . . .

Berggasse 19,
Vienna IX,
11.10.1925
Dear Dr Pfister,
Soon after letting you know about my plan for A.B.[1] a
reaction set in. I began feeling sorry for the poor lad, I had
a change of heart, perhaps I had recovered from a mood of
timidity. In short, I sent you a telegram asking you to do
nothing yet, and decided to take the slower path, that is, to
write directly to his parents. I was very frank with them, and
of my three reasons for thinking of giving up the patient told
them at any rate two: my opinion that he was in need of
treatment that might last for years and that I might not live
to finish it, and my fear that his condition might take a

[1] The young American mentioned in previous letters. Freud had been
thinking of breaking off his analysis for fear of paranoid developments

more serious turn. My third and last motive, that I wanted to spare myself a terrible amount of trouble, I kept to myself. After telling them this, I left them to decide whether to let the lad continue treatment with me or to take him away. If they decided the former, let it be *for better for worse*,[1] without responsibility for possible disturbances on either side. I also initiated them into my plot with you in Zürich, which now, after your explanations, seems to me to be superfluous. I think that thus I have acted for the best, whatever may ensue. Either his parents will take him away, in which case I shall be rid of a difficult and probably thankless task, or, if they let him continue, my position will have been basically strengthened and improved. After the observations in your letter which point to the mother's lack of understanding, the former is the more probable of the two alternatives, and I shall not be sorry.

I find it very flattering that you still have so much confidence in me, but you must admit that it would not be contrary to the course of nature if this time you were wrong. I am tired, as is intelligible after such a troublesome life, and think I have honestly earned rest. The physical components which held together for so long are disintegrating, and who would want to force them to hold together any longer?

I shall keep you duly informed about further developments in the matter of A.B.

With cordial greetings,
Yours,
Freud

PFISTER TO FREUD   *23.12.1925*

One gladly takes refuge from the turmoil of Christmas in the quiet of Bethlehem to rest, reflect and meditate, free from dogma and science. . . . There I derive gladness and strength, and science awakens memory, not of deprivation and hard-

---

[1] These four words in English in the original

ship, but of germinating greatness, succour, and growth. You will smile, but in your neighbourhood too I feel something of the clarity of the Lord, and in any case in thinking of you I am filled with an infinite gratitude and hope. Love is the greatest safeguard against intellectual envy, and after it realisation of the blessing of humility and of the beauty of the honest labour of fetching and carrying, which in the case of your Titanic building is magnificent enough. . . .

Berggasse 19,
Vienna IX,
3.1.1926

Dear Dr Pfister,

Many thanks for having again thought about me at Christmas time. I too am taking advantage of an extension of the holidays to converse with you.

With us the situation, not to say the whole atmosphere, is dominated by Abraham's death which, as you know, took place on Christmas Day. He is a great loss to us, and he will hardly be replaceable. I write that refraining from all emotional reactions and assessing his objective value only. For the time being Eitingon intends to step into the breach and take over his work.

With our lad A.B. things are going very strangely. My belief as a physician that he is on the verge of a paranoid dementia has increased. I was again very near the point of giving him up, but there is something touching about him which deters me from doing so; the threat of breaking off the treatment has made him gentle and amenable again, with the result that at present a good understanding prevails between us. The great deterioration during which the letter to you was written was connected with my telling him the apparently real secret of his neurosis. The immediate reaction to that revelation was bound to be an enormous increase in the resistance. What weighs on me in his case is my belief that, unless the outcome is very good indeed, it will be very bad indeed; what I mean is that he would commit suicide without any hesitation. I shall therefore do all in my power to avert that eventuality.

Thank you for the news about your publications. A new pamphlet of mine, *Inhibitions, Symptoms and Anxiety*, is now being published. It shakes up much that was established and puts things which seemed fixed into a state of flux again. Analysts who above all want peace and certainty will be discontented at having to revise their ideas. But it would be rash to believe that I have now succeeded in finally solving the problem with which the association of anxiety with neurosis confronts us.

This time you do not mention your son, whose development and career interest me greatly.

I send you my cordial greetings and wish you a year full of success and enjoyable work.

Cordially yours,

Freud

PFISTER TO FREUD   *Zürich,*
1.4.1926

... I am taking the opportunity of sending you a just published book about a fashionable Indian miracle worker. You will perhaps be surprised at my taking so much trouble about a sterile subject, and I am even more surprised myself. I wrote an article denouncing the stupid belief people had in the fakir's superhuman claims, with the result that I was attacked, not just as if, like Luther, I had laid hands on the sacred person of the Pope, but as if I had made a bad smell in the Holy of Holies. Now these gentry have got their deserts. The saint is exposed like a prima donna extricated from a stinkbutt and the outcry his fanatical admirers are making is enough to make the devil sick. The freer Protestant circles are delighted at my disclosures. I wanted to strike a blow at superstition, stupidity and goggle-eyed self-abasement, but one should really spend one's time less unprofitably. One makes no real headway against the stink, and the worse the stink the more quickly do worth-while people seek fresh air. I assure you therefore that it is with the greater pleasure that I am returning to the analysis which predominates in the last part of my book. . . .

Berggasse 19,
Vienna IX,
11.4.1926

Dear Dr Pfister,

I like to think of this letter's travelling to Sicily, which is prohibited to me.

I now lie down for an hour every day with a hot water bottle and am using the leisure to read the book about the Christian fakir[1] which your son brought. (I should have liked to have talked to him, but I am now supposed to take a great deal of rest and not see visitors.) The book amused me more than it pleased me. For myself I was glad that I have no religion and therefore do not find myself in the cleft stick which you cannot avoid. So far as you were concerned, I was sorry that you had to busy yourself with such (let us call it) muck. No doubt it will do good in some circles, or you would not have done it. All the same, it is a pity that even you could not be completely honest. You could not possibly count it a virtue of the psychopath that he made such fine speeches, the patterns for which have for a long time been available to all. But that seems to be the whole of his merit.

You will have no difficulty in finding contributors to your new series in Vienna and Berlin; you only have to ask the heads of groups, Dr Simmel[2] and Dr Federn[3] for names.

If you are really still in Sicily when you receive these lines, bear in mind how much pleasure it would give me to be with you.

Yours,
Freud

[1] O. Pfister, *Die Legende Sundar Singhs*, Berne and Leipzig, 1926
[2] Dr Ernst Simmel (1882–1947), director· of the psycho-analytic sanatorium at Tegel, near Berlin; later of Los Angeles
[3] Dr Paul Federn (1872–1950), Vienna psycho-analyst, later of New York

Dear Professor Freud,

I read through your kind gift[1] at one sitting and with great admiration. You have never before written in such a readily comprehensible fashion, yet everything springs from the depths. As one of your first lay pupils, the book gave me unspeakable pleasure. Only *one* lacuna struck me. You mention educational cases, but not the enormous number of adults who are not ill in the medical sense but are nevertheless in extreme need of analysis; I am thinking of alcoholics, people with warped lives, those whose love life has gone astray, frustrated artists, etc. As all these come into the field of the cure of souls, I have a great deal to do with them, and I earnestly appeal to you to cast a benevolent glance at the analytic cure of souls, which is, after all, another of your children. Undoubtedly the cure of souls will one day be a recognised non-ecclesiastical and even non-religious calling. If only men can be made good and happy, with religion or without it, the Lord will assuredly smile approvingly at the work. . . .

It is a great grief to me that the theologians are so backward and wanting. I have now been at work for eighteen years. The educationists have accepted a great deal, and I hear on all sides that analysis is engaging more and more of their interest. But the theologians are too involved in stupid squabbles about principles to care very much about the mental well-being of the laity–or their own. All the same, it has not been all in vain. I am writing an article on Sigmund Freud for the big encyclopaedia *Die Religion in Geschichte und Gegenwart.* . . .

[1] *The Question of Lay Analysis*

Dear Dr Pfister,

I am glad that on the whole you like my pamphlet. But do not judge it as an objective, scientific piece; it is a piece of polemics written for a special occasion. Otherwise I should certainly not have omitted the application of analysis to the cure of souls. I considered doing so, but in Catholic Austria the idea of a 'churchman's' working with analysis is totally inconceivable, and I did not wish further to complicate the issue. Besides, my argument would not have benefited; the answer would have been that, if these spiritual gentlemen wished to use analysis, that was no affair of ours, they should apply for permission to their bishop. I am well aware that Catholic analysis exists in Germany, but it would hardly be possible in Austria.

In regard to your remark about the latency period, let me say that the setting aside of sexuality is often only partial, with the result that a certain amount of activity is maintained. That is very frequent, and there are also plenty of cases with which one would never have hit on the idea of a latency period at all. When one considers the events of the early period, a relative residue of sexual activity is nearly always to be detected. The opposite objection, that in savages there is no latency period, the consequence of which would be that the latter was not innate but a product of civilisation, seems to me to be interesting. I do not believe it to be correct, but the question can be settled only by new and extensive investigations (Malinowski).[1]

I am spending an agreeable time here–so far as my local torment permits–and I propose to prolong it to the end of the month. To-morrow I am sending A.B., who has been here since August 1, on holiday until October 1. I must tell you about him, there have been a good many changes in his case. His intolerableness has been successfully overcome, I have actually grown fond of him, and he seems to reciprocate this.

[1] Bronislaw Malinowski (1881–1942), British anthropologist

After dreadful difficulties some pieces of the secret history of his development have been laid bare, and the effect, as was corroborated by relatives who saw him during the holidays, has been very favourable. Outwardly he still behaves strangely enough and is still very far from normal, as is in accordance with the incompleteness of our results. On the other hand it is undeniable that there is a great deal about him that is alarming, as if he were on the way to passing from obsessional neurosis to paranoia. There is often a very strange quality about his ideas and chains of thought, and his symptoms could without much difficulty be called delusions. Whenever he succumbs to resistance I tell myself that it is a case of schizophrenia after all, but that impression vanishes when something is cleared up. I propose to leave aside the academic question of diagnosis and go on working with the living material. So long as this remains plastic and we have successes, I feel this is justified. A not inessential factor is the impression that his personality is worth any amount of trouble.

With cordial greeting, and in the hope of soon hearing again about your work.

Yours,
Freud

Berggasse 19,
Vienna IX,
21.11.1926

Dear Dr Pfister,

Let me congratulate you. I shall gladly set aside a special shelf for the translations of your books if you send me them. Of all the applications of psycho-analysis the only one that is really flourishing is that initiated by you in the field of education. It gives me great pleasure that my daughter is beginning to do good work in that field.

The day after receiving your book I dreamt I was in Zürich. Evidently I wanted to come and see you – the dream of a man whose infirmities prevent him from travelling. At Christmas I want to try and go to Berlin—to make the acquaintance of four small grandchildren.[1]

Cordially yours,

Freud

Berggasse 19,
Vienna IX,
11.4.1927

Dear Dr Pfister,

Thank you for your autobiographical sketch[2] and the complementary accompanying poem, which obviously accords with your idea of your outer ego. I read the prose carefully, and in doing so surveyed your whole development in my mind. Permit me to express one surprising thing that struck me in retrospect in regard to the first edition of your *Psycho-Analytic Method*. This was that you put up so much better resistance to the confusion of Jung than you did to the absurdity of Adler. To you love is the salvation of the world and the core of religion, but nevertheless you hesitated for a time in the face of a theory which denies love and admits no motive but self-assertion. Your dubiety in the matter fortunately belongs to the past, and I return to it now only because I still detect an echo of it in your present attitude to instinct theory. It is not correct that the instincts are *never* found in isolation; there are reactions in which one finds only one or only the other; and even if they never appeared in isolation that would be no reason for not distinguishing between them. Gold never occurs in nature without an admixture of silver and copper, but that is no reason for not recognising the essential differences between them. But I am in a very morose mood to-day, my prosthesis is tormenting me.

I gave your autobiographical sketch to A.B. to read, and

---

[1] Three sons of Ernst and a daughter of Oliver

[2] O. Pfister, *Die Pädagogik der Gegenwart in Selbstdarstellungen*, Felix Meinert, Leipzig, 1927

the unfavourable reaction showed me how little I have accomplished with him. He has not yet given up his childish reactions to the influence of authority, and it is that that makes him so difficult to treat. I am not wasting time on the question of correct diagnosis; he certainly has plenty of schizophrenic traits, without there being any need to send him away for that reason. After all, it is not very clear what that diagnosis means. But the lad is a severe ordeal. I am trying hard to get him deliberately to resist his fetishist masturbation to enable him to corroborate for himself all that I have discerned about the nature of the fetish, but he will not believe that such abstinence will lead to this and is essential for the progress of the treatment. On the other hand I feel a great deal of sympathy for him, and cannot make up my mind to send him away and risk a disastrous outcome. So I am continuing with him, though perhaps if I give up work he will leave me in any case.

I know that your jubilee in the church is imminent. Allow me, though prematurely, to be one of those who will congratulate you.

With cordial greetings,
Yours,
Freud

Berggasse 19,
Vienna IX,
1.6.1927

Dear Dr Pfister,

I have just finished the hangman's job you asked me to do *via* Frau H. The letters of 1912 have been destroyed; a few of impersonal content still remain.

I have done what you asked me to do, but did not do so gladly. I regretted the letters, which I read again for the first time after so many years. I pictured you in my mind as you were then, with all your winning characteristics, your enthusiasm, your exuberant gratitude, your courageous integrity, the way you blossomed forth after your first contact with analysis, as well as your blessed confidence in people who were so soon to disappoint you. And, though you were also at that time in danger of committing stupidities, and since then fate has dealt more kindly with you, I could not help feeling regret that that battle passed you by; and perhaps it was not just my fanaticism or the spectator's desire for sensation that made me feel like that; friendship also perhaps had something to do with it.

I have just re-read the letter in which you wrote to me: 'Do not talk of your age, you are the youngest of us all'. Would you still write that to-day?

I greet you cordially,
Yours,
Freud

Berggasse 19,
Vienna IX,
16.10.1927

Dear Dr Pfister,

Thanks to your letters, I have been following with intelligible interest your triumphal progress through the Scandinavian countries. The very gratifying result must largely be attributed to your personality, because the resistance to analysis of these Scandinavians is particularly deep-rooted.

In regard to your Swedish friend's book on asceticism,[1] please get in touch with Dr Eitingon, who is now in charge of the publishing house. You know in what straits that institution of ours now is. In view of that a recommendation from me would carry no weight.

In the next few weeks a pamphlet of mine[2] will be appearing which has a great deal to do with you. I had been wanting to write it for a long time, and postponed it out of regard for you, but the impulse became too strong. The subject-matter

---

[1] Christian Schjelderup, *Die Askese*, Walter de Gruyter, Berlin, 1928
[2] *The Future of an Illusion*, Standard Ed. Vol. XXI

– as you will easily guess – is my completely negative attitude to religion, in any form and however attenuated, and, though there can be nothing new to you in this, I feared, and still fear, that such a public profession of my attitude will be painful to you. When you have read it you must let me know what measure of toleration and understanding you are able to preserve for the hopeless pagan.

Always your cordially devoted

Freud

PFISTER TO FREUD   *Zürich,*
21.10.1927

. . . As for your anti-religious pamphlet, there is nothing new to me in your rejection of religion. I look forward to it with pleasurable anticipation. A powerful-minded opponent of religion is certainly of more service to it than a thousand useless supporters. In music, philosophy, and religion I go different ways from you. I have been unable to imagine that a public profession of what you believe could be painful to me; I have always believed that every man should state his honest opinion aloud and plainly. You have always been tolerant towards me, and am I to be intolerant of your atheism? If I frankly air my differences from you, you will certainly not take it amiss. Meanwhile my attitude is one of eager curiosity.

Permit me to mention an entirely different matter. It concerns what you describe as the unsolved problem of therapy. It appears that F. gained no lasting help from analysis in Vienna. He describes the therapeutic success of the analysis as minimal, and regards it all as theory. And here is a quite different experience. Harald Schjelderup, a brilliant thirty-two-year-old professor of philosophy and psychology, who wrote the first analytically oriented psychological text-book – it is due soon to appear in German – was under analysis with Dr H. for seven months, during which his agonising weekly migraines grew worse and worse, until he had to return to Oslo.

Well, this summer he came to me. We analysed hard, and the last, much milder, attack took place after a fortnight. After that we went on analysing for about another three weeks, but the originally violent pathogenic repressions made no further appearance, and after three weeks we broke off. Then, without our doing any more analysis, after the Locarno congress he accompanied me to Zermatt. Since the beginning of July the migraines have disappeared completely. Schjelderup's attitude to Dr H. was not bad, but predominantly negative. He wrote to me as follows about the difference in method:

I believe the time I spent with you will be of great importance to my whole future. I went through an analysis with Dr H., but had the impression that the difference between your method and his was very great. The difference is not only that you do much more interpreting and by your interpretations advance, not only towards the general instinctual drives, but also to the particular conflict situations. The whole nature of your analysis is much more active and effective. There was something unsatisfactory about the whole analysis in Vienna, and something humiliating to one's ego feeling as well. When an unpleasing instinctual impulse or infantile wish appeared, I was left with no idea what to do with it; the fact was simply noted. But you laid emphasis on your own attitude and on its connections with the whole. It seems to me that only if that is done can inappropriate attitudes be really disposed of. Thereby the humiliating element in the situation largely disappears, and a healthy transference is made possible. . . . I have the definite impression that the short time I spent with you was of much more practical value than the seven months' analysis in Vienna. The migraine has gone–I hope for ever.

I had similar experiences with the brother of the writer of this letter, whose career was wrecked by inappropriate treatment and, in spite of enormous gifts, which his latest book brilliantly corroborates, got into incredible difficulties, like Strindberg's stepson, a student who developed a headache after working for an hour and was practically unable to work at all, with the result that after five years' 'work' he had got nowhere at all, as has happened to many others.

With the exception of a few cases which ended unsatisfactorily, I have never experienced dependence or lasting over-affection on the part of my patients, but only a certain attitude of gratitude and liking, which seems to me healthier and more natural than just a cold leave-taking from a person to whom, after all, one has so much to be grateful for. After all, behind the personal relations springing from the transference in the narrower sense for which there is no justification in reality there must be real relations based on the real characteristics of the two persons concerned. Should the attitude to the analyst not be a pattern for what it should to other people? ... I am really not concerned with making friends of my analysands, but for their good; hence this is a therapeutic question. In your paper on *The Ego and the Id* you mention in the footnote on page 64 the importance of the analyst's personality's permitting him to take the place of the patient's ego-ideal. I should like to add that, according to my observations, it is also important that the analyst should transmit values which over-compensate for the patient's gain from illness or guilt feelings.

Thus my question is: Do you feel it is a difference between us that I do not completely break the link with the patient, but only cleanse the transference of all unreality? You will no doubt approve of my being always ready to be of assistance in making use of every kind of human value in regard to which the patient is not always able to help himself, because that is my duty as an educator and a minister. ...

Berggasse 19,
Vienna IX,
22.10.1927

Dear Dr Pfister,
Such is your magnanimity that I expected no other answer to my 'declaration of war'. The prospect of your making a public stand against my pamphlet gives me positive pleasure, it will be refreshing in the discordant critical chorus

for which I am prepared. We know that by different routes we aspire to the same objectives for poor humanity.

On the question of therapeutic technique I must express myself plainly. You as a minister naturally have the right to call on all the reinforcements at your command, while we as analysts must be more reserved, and must lay the chief accent on the effort to make the patient independent, which often works out to the disadvantage of the therapy. Apart from that, I am not so far from your point of view as you think. You know the human propensity to take precepts literally or exaggerate them. I know very well that in the matter of analytic passivity that is what some of my pupils do. Of H. in particular I am willing to believe that he spoils the effect of analysis by a certain listless indifference, and then neglects to lay bare the resistances which he thereby awakens in his patients. It should not be concluded from this instance that analysis should be followed by a synthesis, but rather that thorough analysis of the transference situation is of special importance. What then remains of the transference may, indeed should, have the character of a cordial human relationship.

A.B. undoubtedly has very many paranoid traits–but we can continue the work not without good hopes.

With cordial greetings,

Yours,

Freud

PFISTER TO FREUD   *Zürich,*
24.II.27

Dear Professor Freud,

If I express my sincere thanks for the warmth of your dedication, please do not regard it merely as a conventional reaction to a friendly gift. That you care for me a little gives me uncommon pleasure and makes me almost a little proud. As for what I think of your work, it is exactly as I foresaw. If anything surprised me, it is that I was so little surprised.

You have the right to expect complete frankness from me, and you know that neither my attitude to you nor my pleasure in psycho-analysis is in the slightest degree diminished by your rejection of religion. I have always emphasised that psycho-analysis is the most fruitful part of psychology, but is not the whole of the science of the mind, and still less a philosophy of life and the world. You are certainly of the same view.

I cannot have things out with you properly on the subject of religion because you completely reject philosophy, approach art in a way that differs from mine, and regard morality as something self-evident. I can understand an important natural scientist like Driesch,[1] who went over to philosophy after a long and successful career in experimental research, much better than one who merely abides by the data. 'Pure' experience is in my view a fiction in any event, and if we look at the history of the sciences we see how doubtful is the reality hidden behind our so-called experience. And even this mixture of illusion and truth that we call 'experience' we acquire only with the aid of trans-empirical assumptions. Conceptions such as causality, the aether, the atom, etc., are certainly saturated with much bigger contradictions than those of the theologians, and you know better than I do how natural laws have been uprooted by present-day physics. In my view there can be no such thing as a pure empiricist, and a man who sticks rigidly to the data is like a heart specialist who ignores the organism as a whole and its invisible laws, divisions of function, etc. Thus I have to find a place for the unconscious in mental life as a whole, and for the latter in society, the universe, and its trans-empirical realities. For this in the first place I require a theory of perception. If error is liable to creep into this, the same in your own opinion applies to you.

What you say about the contradictions of religious and theological thought you yourself describe as a repetition, a

[1] Hans Driesch (1867–1941), Professor of Philosophy in Cologne and later Leipzig

repetition psycho-analytically developed in depth, of long familiar ideas. But what surprises me is that you pay no regard to the voices of those defenders of religion who bring out those contradictions just as sharply and resolve them in a higher philosophical-religious context. Let me mention von Eucken, *Der Wahrheitsgehalt der Religion*, first edition, p. 274 *ff*. Also Brunstäd, *Die Idee der Religion*, p. 256*ff*., concerns himself with conflicting values, and it is significant that deeply intelligent men have gone over from philosophy to theology. My friend Albert Schweitzer, the distinguished philosopher, professor of theology, organ virtuoso, etc., thinks just as pessimistically as you do about the optimistic-ethical interpretation of the world (*Kultur und Ethik*, Introduction, p. xiii); but in his view that is only the beginning of the real problem, and he does not shut himself off from insight into the philosophy of life of those without a philosophy of life. (*Verfall und Wiederaufbau der Kultur*, p. 53.)

Your substitute for religion is basically the idea of the eighteenth-century Enlightenment in proud modern guise. I must confess that, with all my pleasure in the advance of science and technique, I do not believe in the adequacy and sufficiency of that solution of the problem of life. It is very doubtful whether, taking everything into account, scientific progress has made men happier or better. According to the statistics, there are more criminals among scholars than in the intellectual middle class, and the hopes that were set on universal education have turned out to be illusory. Nietzsche summed up your position in the words:

The reader will have realised my purport; namely that there is always a metaphysical belief on which our belief in science rests —that we observers of to-day, atheists and anti-metaphysicians as we are, still draw our fire from the blaze lit by a belief thousands of years old, the Christian belief, which was also that of Plato, that God is truth and that the truth is divine. . . . But supposing that this grew less and less believable and nothing divine was left, save error, blindness, lies?

I do not properly understand your outlook on life. It is

impossible that what you reject as the end of an illusion and value as the sole truth can be all. A world without temples, the fine arts, poetry, religion, would in my view be a devil's island to which men could have been banished, not by blind chance, but only by Satan. In that case your pessimism about the wickedness of mankind would be much too mild; you would have to follow it through to its logical conclusion. If it were part of psycho-analytic treatment to present that despoiled universe to our patients as the truth, I should well understand it if the poor devils preferred remaining shut up in their illness to entering that dreadful icy desolation.

Have you as much tolerance for this frank profession of faith as I have for your long-familiar heresies? I hold it as a piece of good fortune that you had to deprive yourself of so much in order to do such tremendous work in your science (with which your faith or lack of faith has nothing whatever to do). But allow me to add two questions. Would you agree to my dealing with your views in *Imago*? Perhaps I might be able to offer a little aid to many who now, according to your own expectation, run the risk of rejecting the whole of psycho-analysis, and thus I might be doing a service to the psycho-analytic movement. . . .

Thus there remains between us the great difference that I practise analysis within a plan of life which you indulgently regard as servitude to my calling, while I regard this philosophy of life, not only as a powerful aid to treatment (in the case of most people), but also as the logical consequence of a philosophy that goes beyond naturalism and positivism, is well based on moral and social hygiene, and is in accordance with the nature of mankind and the world. In all this it is the patient's business to what extent he will strike out on a road in harmony with his social and individual characteristics, and the amount of aid he requires to find what is the right road for him depends on himself alone.

Well, I have come to the end of a long letter. In writing it I have had your picture in front of me, listening to what I said with indulgence and friendliness. I hope that speaking out like this has only strengthened our friendship. It has, has it not?

With cordial greetings,
Yours,
Pfister

Berggasse 19,
Vienna IX,
26.11.1927

Dear Dr Pfister,

You were quite right, there was no room for any surprises; you were prepared for what I had to say, and I for your disagreement. I might have been tempted to point out that the argument you are using is: This must be wrong because accepting it as the truth it would be too unpleasant, and that the difficulties of my position do nothing to strengthen yours. But that would not forward the argument, and would be only a repetition, because it is already in the little book, so I prefer to go on to your two questions, both of which are of practical importance.

To the best of my belief, we have already made up our minds on one of them. I attach importance to your publishing your criticism – in *Imago*, if you like – and I hope that in it you will specifically draw attention to our undisturbed friendship and your unshaken loyalty to analysis. Your second question involves issues which perhaps had better be separated out. Let us be quite clear on the point that the views expressed in my book form no part of analytic theory. They are my personal views, which coincide with those of many non-analysts and pre-analysts, but there are certainly many excellent analysts who do not share them. If I drew on analysis for certain arguments – in reality only one argument – that need deter no-one from using the non-partisan method of analysis for arguing the opposite view. That too is mentioned in the little book. If it were argued that that was not so easy, for the practice of analysis necessarily led to the abandonment of religion, the reply would be that that was no less true of any other science.

The other issue, that of influencing analytic therapy by granting or refusing an illusory emotional satisfaction is, strictly speaking, irrelevant, because, however warm-heartedly the analyst may behave, he cannot set himself up in the analysand's mind as a substitute for God and providence. If your authority complains about the dry tracing back of his aspirations to the father-son relationship, it must be pointed out to him that the analyst cannot satisfy this aspiration, but must leave it to the analysand either to overcome it after the explanation has been given to him or to satisfy it in a religious or any other sublimated fashion. The analyst can of course make a bad technical mistake if he creates the impression of belittling this emotional demand, or calls on everyone to overcome a piece of infantilism which only a few are capable of overcoming.

The whole question is of great importance and requires a cool all-round assessment. Whether you will undertake it in connection with your criticism of the *Illusion* is a matter on which I do not want to influence you.

With cordial greetings,

Yours,

Freud

P.S. As you quoted statements by a number of important men on our problem, you will certainly be interested in what Bleuler wrote to me:

> I promptly devoured your *Future of an Illusion* and enjoyed it. Starting from quite different standpoints one comes to the identical conclusion, but your argument is not only particularly elegant, it of course goes to the heart of the matter. There is only one point on which I cannot agree with you. In your book civilisation and morality merge into a single concept, or at any rate the boundaries between them are largely obliterated. I cannot help making a sharp distinction between the two.

Berggasse 19,
Vienna IX,
11.1.1928

Dear Dr Pfister,

The rumour of what has been going on with you had already reached me by a private route. Thank you very much for your detailed information. It will be Eitingon's task to deal with the matter, officially I have nothing to do with it. However, I shall gladly tell you what my personal attitude is.

I am opposed to all lame compromises, would never take any trouble to keep anyone who wanted to leave, and would never accept such a suspect formula as formal association. Whether two Swiss societies[1] are possible within the framework of our organisation is a matter for the committee to decide. My vote goes in favour of the society in which Pfister, Sarasin[2] and Zulliger are active.

Your reply in *Imago* is awaited with interest. Men's real allegiance is shown in difficult times.

With cordial greetings,
Yours,
Freud

Berggasse 19,
Vienna IX,
18.1.1928

Dear Dr Pfister,

I am glad you have sent me H.'s war-whoop. Thus I have the opportunity to be astonished at it and to recognise it as a huge pretext. A difference of opinion about the value of analytic therapy is no sort of reason for aspiring to a purely formal membership of our association. But what is especially surprising about the excuse chosen is that it is based on nothing recent. In recent years, I believe, I have made very few utteranecs on the subject of therapy either verbally or in print, and

---

[1] The Swiss Psycho-Analytic Society, unlike some others, accepted non-medical members

[2] Philipp Sarasin, b. 1888, Swiss psycho-analyst

since my illness I have not been to the Vienna society, at which I am alleged to have said such wounding things about the therapists. Moreover, on this point of therapy there has been little change or development in me, and I still think what I thought and said many years ago. What that was I will gladly summarise for you. You will see that there is nothing in it to force anyone to resign from the international association.

I am just as opposed to under-estimating the value of our therapy as I am to over-estimating it. I have claimed that the successes of analysis have nothing to be ashamed of in comparison with those of physical medicine, and that analysis does everything that can be demanded of a therapy *at the present time*. On the other hand, I have also stated that we must recognise its limitations. Its chief defect resides in the fact that the quantities of energy that we mobilise through the analysis are not always of the order of magnitude of those warring with each other in the neurotic conflict. As a still hazy future possibility we may hope that endocrinology will provide us with the means of influencing this quantitative factor, in which event analysis will retain the merit of having shown the way to this organic therapy.

Also I have often said that I hold that the purely medical importance of analysis is outweighed by its importance to science as a whole, and that its general influence by means of clarification and the exposure of error exceeds its therapeutic value to the individual.

What I shall think about these things in ten years' time I do not know – I hope it will be nothing at all – but H. does not know either.

I naturally agree to your making any use of this letter that you may think fit, and am glad to hear that prospects look so favourable in the matter.

Cordially, and with greetings to all our friends,

Yours,

Freud

Berggasse 19,
Vienna IX,
17.2.1928

Dear Dr Pfister,

I have received a detailed memorandum from H. in which he tries to justify his step. Neither his previous behaviour towards us nor his present procedure against the International Psycho-Analytical Association and the non-physicians are made more intelligible thereby, and I have written to him to that effect.

On the other hand I have been very sorry to hear what a large part was played in his departure by critical dissatisfaction with your analytic practices and your therapeutical optimism. Sorry, because on these points I am to a large extent on his side and, with all my personal liking for you and all my appreciation of your work, I cannot approve of your enthusiastically abbreviated analyses and the ease with which you accept new members and followers. I should prefer not to choose between you, but to keep both of you with your failings and your bluntnesses, and I should like you to get on with and become more moderate towards each other. Permit me to hope that this wish is not unfulfillable, and that you will find your way to it.

With cordial greetings,
Yours,
Freud

PFISTER TO FREUD

Zürich,
20.2.28

Dear Professor Freud,

This is the third week I have been in bed, and I am very annoyed that no-one has purloined and made off with my phlebitis. I have been using the rest chiefly to write my friendly criticism of you. I have been doing so with the greater pleasure because in it I do battle for a cause that is dear to me with an opponent who is the same. There is not much danger of your turning up for baptism or of my descending from the pulpit, but among the points that bring us closer to each other there are some which are very important, and when I reflect that you are much better and deeper than your disbelief, and that I am much worse and more superficial than my faith, I conclude that the abyss between us cannot yawn so grimly. While I wrote I saw your picture smiling indulgently at me, but all the same I felt in a very glad mood. I very much hope that you will not take amiss what I have to say; I even hope that in spite of my friendly attack on you you will derive a tiny little bit of pleasure from it.

I am sending you the manuscript to give you the opportunity of letting me know if anything strikes you as unsuitable for publication, or if you think I have done you an injustice on any point.

Our difference derives chiefly from the fact that you grew up in proximity to pathological forms of religion and regard these as 'religion', while I had the good fortune of being able to turn to a free form of religion which to you seems to be an emptying of Christianity of its content, while I regard it as the core and substance of evangelism. . . .

Berggasse 19,
Vienna IX,
24.2.1928

Dear Dr Pfister,

It is very unfair of fate to send you to your bed with phlebitis. Your active way of life, your mountain-climbing, should have assured your circulation better than that. But when is fate not unfair?

That provides the transition to your reply to me. It has already gone to the editorial office. It was very necessary that my *Illusion* should be answered from within our own circle, and it is very satisfactory that it should be done in such a worthy and friendly fashion.

What the effect on me was of what you have to say you

have no need to ask. What is to be expected if one is judge in one's own cause? Some of your arguments seem to me to be poetical effusion, others, such as the enumeration of great minds who have believed in God, too cheap. It is unreasonable to expect science to produce a system of ethics – ethics are a kind of highway code for traffic among mankind – and the fact that in physics atoms which were yesterday assumed to be square are now assumed to be round is exploited with unjustified tendentiousness by all who are hungry for faith; so long as physics extends our dominion over nature, these changes ought to be a matter of complete indifference to you. And finally – let me be impolite for once – how the devil do you reconcile all that we experience and have to expect in this world with your assumption of a moral world order? I am curious about that, but you have no need to reply.

I am passing on to Eitingon your very friendly letter to H. It does great credit to your character. Only it reminds me of the last joke of my 'fellow in disbelief' Heine – the phrase is his too – who, when the priest assured him that God would forgive him, replied: *Bien sûr qu'il me pardonnera, c'est son métier*. If I were able to treat a stubborn opponent as you treat H. I should be proud of myself, but the fact that you have to do so disturbs me. I have little confidence that you will get anywhere with the stiff-necked fellow. Incidentally, it is extraordinary how difficult it is to establish the facts of a situation beyond any possibility of doubt, even when those concerned are such decent people as you and, no doubt, H. are.

But enough of all such profundities. I regress to the unspeakably stupid but universal assumption of the omnipotence of thoughts and wish you a speedy recovery and resurrection.

Cordially,
Yours,
Freud

POSTCARD   *Semmering,*
                                                  30.7.1928
Dear Dr Pfister,

My congratulations on your trial of strength.[1] A few days
ago I myself was up on the Rax (6,000 feet), which a few
decades ago I used to climb three times a week (see Katharina
in *Studies on Hysteria*, 1895), but this time it was with the help
of the cable railway.

Sic transit and *tempora mutantur.*

                                                  Cordially yours,
                                                  Freud

PFISTER TO FREUD   *Zürich,*
                                                  16.11.1928

... I have been very impressed at the attitude of the International Society's journal in the debate on *The Future of an
Illusion.* Such non-partisanship is very creditable. If our opponents always tell us that analysts are pettier and more spite-
ful, more intolerant and more fanatical, than the unanalysed,
this debate refutes them. To me the tussle with you has been
stimulating and helpful. Let me again thank you cordially
for your kindness. ...

As you have been kind enough to deal with my questions
and diminish my ignorance, I am taking the liberty of again
putting a question to you. In your *Three Essays on the Theory on
Sexuality* (v, 41), you talk of qualityless instincts which receive
their specific characteristics only from their somatic sources
and aims. Are these specific characteristics still unconscious
as pertaining to the id? The qualityless instincts seem to me
to be very important in establishing the organic unity of the
individual and avoiding the impression that you think of this
as being put together like a mosaic.

My other question concerns technique. When one returns
to interpretations one has given, one continually finds that
under the influence of the resistance the patient's memory has

[1] Pfister had climbed the Matterhorn

distorted what one said, with the result that wrong ideas are firmly planted in his mind and attributed to the analyst. With some analysands I have dictated summaries with very successful results, with others I have analysed the distorted interpretations, but with others again this did not succeed, as for instance, with our A.B., who did not assimilate the dictated version either. Do you think my experiments inappropriate? . . .

Berggasse 19,
Vienna IX,
25.11.1928

Dear Dr Pfister,

In your otherwise delightful letter there is one point I cavil at, namely your finding something surprising and gratifying in the attitude of the International Journal (editor and staff) on the subject of the *Illusion*.[1] Such 'tolerance' is no merit.

In both works which have recently reached me from the publishing house, one of which contains a reprint of your *Discussion*,[2] I note with satisfaction what a long way we are able to go together in analysis. The rift, not in analytic, but in scientific thinking which one comes on when the subject of God and Christ is touched on I accept as one of the logically untenable but psychologically only too intelligible irrationalities of life. In general I attach no value to the 'imitation of Christ'. In contrast to utterances as psychologically profound as 'Thy sins are forgiven thee; arise and walk' there are a large number of others which are conditioned exclusively by the time, psychologically impossible, useless for our lives. Besides, the above statement calls for analysis. If the sick man had asked: 'How knowest thou that my sins are forgiven?' the answer could only have been: 'I, the Son of God, forgive thee'. In other words, a call for unlimited transference. And now, just suppose I said to a patient: 'I, Professor Sigmund Freud, forgive thee thy sins'. What a fool I should make of myself. To

---

[1] O. Pfister, *Die Illusion einer Zukunft*, Imago, 1928 [2] Title not identifiable

the former case the principle applies that analysis is not satisfied with success produced by suggestion, but investigates the origin of and justification for the transference.

I do not understand the first of your two questions. I do not see what connection there can be between the lack of quality of component instincts and the question of their consciousness or unconsciousness, and I have never understood what you call the 'mosaic', or why you are afraid of it. To your second question I can reply with complete confidence that such attempts to fix the results of analysis intellectually have no technical value, as frequent experience has demonstrated.

Your account of your unsuccessful case raises an interesting problem. It really does happen that, in contrast to the usual state of affairs, the conscience, the better, the 'nobler' impulses suffer repression instead of the instinctually 'wicked' and unacceptable. Dynamically that seems to present no difficulties, but must depend on special conditions which have not been investigated.

I do not know if you have detected the secret link between the *Lay Analysis* and the *Illusion*. In the former I wish to protect analysis from the doctors and in the latter from the priests. I should like to hand it over to a profession which does not yet exist, a profession of *lay* curers of souls who need not be doctors and should not be priests.

Cordially,
Your old friend,
Freud

PFISTER TO FREUD   *Zürich*,
                                          9.2.29
... Please allow me to return to your remark that the analysts you would like to see should not be priests. It seems to me that analysis as such must be a purely 'lay' affair. By its very nature it is essentially private and directly yields no higher values. In innumerable cases I have done nothing but this negative work, without ever mentioning a word about

religion. The Good Samaritan also preached no sermons, and it would be tasteless to have a successful treatment paid for in retrospect by religious obligations. Just as Protestantism abolished the difference between laity and clergy, so must the cure of souls be laicised and secularised. Even the most bigoted must admit that the love of God is not limited by the whiff of incense.

However, it seems to me that not only children but adults very frequently have an inner need of positive values of a spiritual nature, of ethics and a philosophy of life, and these, as Hartmann[1] has recently so elegantly demonstrated, psychoanalysis cannot supply. Indeed, there are many who need ethical considerations, which they are not willing to modify merely by way of the transference, in order to be able to cope with their pathogenic moral conflicts. If no priest should analyse, neither should any Christian or any religious or morally deep-thinking individual, and you yourself emphasise that analysis is independent of philosophy of life. Disbelief is after all nothing but a negative belief. I do not believe that psycho-analysis eliminates art, philosophy, religion, but that it helps to purify and refine them. Forgive a long-standing enthusiast for art and humanitarianism and an old servant of God. Your marvellous life's work and your goodness and gentleness, which are somehow an incarnation of the meaning of existence, lead me to the deepest springs of life. I am not content to do scientific research on their banks, but have to drink and draw strength from them. Goethe's *Wenn ihr's nicht fühlt, ihr könnt es nicht erjagen*[2] is still valid, and will always be. At school my cleverest master used to say that music was a pitiful row. I did not try to convert him, but took refuge in Beethoven and Schubert. At heart you serve exactly the same purpose as I, and act 'as if' there were a purpose and meaning in life and the universe, and I with my feeble powers can only fit your brilliant analytical discoveries and healing powers into that gap. Do you really wish to exclude

[1] Dr Heinz Hartmann, formerly of Vienna, now of New York
[2] 'If you cannot feel it, you will never lay hold of it'

from analytical work a 'priesthood' understood in this sense? I do not believe that that is what you mean. . . .

Berggasse 19,
Vienna IX,
16.2.1929

Dear Dr Pfister,

I have discussed with Anna the possibility of her attending the congress at Elsinore[1] (August 8–22), but found her very loth, I think with good reason. She has to give a lecture in Frankfurt very soon, she is going with me to Berlin in March, is meeting Eitingon, Jones and Ferenczi in Paris in April, and of course cannot miss the conference at Oxford,[2] so you will see that she has enough travel in store for this year and is reluctant still further to restrict the summer after a hard year's work. With Aichhorn[3] it would be different, I mean it would be if I had not already spoken to him, there would be nothing to stop his travelling. But I know that he is an official who lives on a limited budget and cannot afford the expense of such a journey. Also I wonder whether you do not over-estimate the importance of this congress and its attitude to analysis. In one eventuality I should myself embark on the trip to Elsinore in spite of all my infirmities, that is, if you could persuade Prince Hamlet to appear in person and confess in a lecture that he indeed suffered from the Oedipus complex, which so many people refuse to believe. But even you will not be able to manage that, so I shall have to stay at home.

My remark that the analysts of my phantasy of the future should not be priests does not sound very tolerant, I admit. But you must consider that I was referring to a very distant future. For the present I put up with doctors, so why not

[1] World Conference on New Education
[2] The eleventh psycho-analytical congress
[3] August Aichhorn, Viennese educationist and psycho-analyst (1878–1949)

priests too? You are quite right to point out that analysis leads to no new philosophy of life, but it has no need to, for it rests on the general scientific outlook, with which the religious outlook is incompatible. For the point of view of the latter it is immaterial whether Christ, Buddha, or Confucius is regarded as the ideal of human conduct and held up as an example to imitate. Its essence is the pious illusion of providence and a moral world order, which are in conflict with reason. But priests will remain bound to stand for them. It is of course possible to take advantage of the human right to be irrational and go some way with analysis and then stop, rather on the pattern of Charles Darwin, who used to go regularly to church on Sundays. I cannot honestly see that any difficulties are created by patients' demands for ethical values; ethics are not based on an external world order but on the inescapable exigencies of human cohabitation. I do not believe that I behave as if there were 'one life, one meaning in life,' that was an excessively friendly thought on your part, and it always reminds me of the monk who insisted on regarding Nathan as a thoroughly good Christian. I am a long way from being Nathan, but of course I cannot help remaining 'good' towards you.

Cordially yours,
Freud

Berggasse 19,
Vienna IX,
23.2.1929

Dear Dr Pfister,

I know how lonely you must feel now that such a long period of life together has been cut short,[1] and in all friendship and sympathy I clasp your hand.

Yours,
Freud

[1] The reference is to the death of Pfister's first wife

Dear Dr Pfister,

So far you are the only one whom I have not thanked for sending me birthday greetings. Now I do so, and I am glad that it is done. Life is in any case not easy, its value is doubtful, and having to be grateful for reaching the age of seventy-three seems to be one of those unfairnesses which my friend Pfister puts up with better than I. However, if you promise never to do it again, I shall once more forgive you, just as you seem to forgive me a lot of things, including *The Future of an Illusion.*

With cordial greetings,

Yours,

Freud

PFISTER TO FREUD *Zürich,*
4.2.30

. . . Please forgive me for having delayed so long acknowledging your kindness in sending me your book on civilisation and its discontents. You will certainly have attributed this to my discontent with it, but I must add that I have also derived from it a great deal of pleasure. I recall that nearly twenty years ago (if I am not mistaken) you wrote to me that you looked forward with dread to the time when your mental powers would fade. Now you have left seventy well behind, and your freshness is enriching and invigorating. You would live on a lonely height if you were only a thinker, for who would there be to compare you with? But you live in the midst of a circle of living, venerating, grateful men because, in spite of your pessimism, you are full of kindness and benevolence.

I gladly make use of the opportunity freely to criticise your book. Years ago I read in Ebbinghaus's text-book of psychology: 'The analysis of love-life leads to nothing but trivialities' (Vol. II, p. 346). That is what I feel in reading your new little book, which contains a tremendous number of deep and important ideas but, so it seems to me, is not right in everything. I cannot go into details or the result would be a treatise, but allow me just a few generalisations. In instinctual theory you are a conservative while I am a progressive. As in the biological theory of evolution, I see an upward trend, as in Spitteler's Olympian spring, in which the laborious ascent of the gods continues, in spite of obstacles and reverses and occasional slippings back. I regard the 'death instinct', not as a real instinct, but only as a slackening of the 'life force', and even the death of the individual cannot hold up the advance of the universal will, but only help it forward. I see civilisation as full of tensions. Just as in the individual with his free will there is a conflict between the present and the future to which he aspires, so is it with civilisation. Just as it would be mistaken to regard the actual, existing facts about an individual as the whole of him, ignoring his aspirations, it would be equally mistaken to identify with civilisation its existing horrors, to which its magnificent achievements stand out in contrast.

In my paper on psycho-analysis and philosophy of life I described ethics as a hygienic measure (perhaps I was the first to do so). I regard them not only as therapeutic (*Civilisation and its Discontents*, p. 133)[1] but also as prophylactic, though by that I think I have dealt with the matter only in part. Just as doctor, employer, teacher, etc., are important in the life of the individual, so are individual and social hygiene as important in the life of civilisation as they are in that of the individual.

Reading your book is like travelling through a mountain landscape. Here a ravine opens into which one cannot see, but there a wide valley opens up. Many a brief phrase tempts one to explore further, and one is certain to come upon important *terra incognita*. . . .

[1] Standard Ed. Vol. XXI, p. 142

Dear Dr Pfister,

Outside it is raining, we cannot take Wolf[1] for his usual morning walk because his inclination to eczema means that he must not get wet, and so I have an hour's time in which to answer your letter of yesterday without delay.

All the news that you give about yourself is not glad news, but what right have we to expect that everything should be glad? At any rate I am glad that you write about yourself and your work, your hopes and griefs. At a distance it is so easy to drift apart if one does not keep in touch, and there is a special value in personal relations which shared work and interests cannot completely make good; and we two, at this moment when we have become aware of the ultimate, fundamental differences between us, have particular occasion – and, I hope, inclination – to foster such relations.

You are right in saying that my mental powers have not dwindled with my surplus years (over seventy). Though they show the influence of age plainly enough. There are three ways of disintegration between which nature takes her choice in individual cases – simultaneous destruction of mind and body, premature mental decay accompanied by physical preservation, and survival of mental life accompanied by physical decrepitude; and in my case it is the third and most merciful of these which has set in. Very well, then, I shall take advantage of this favourable circumstance to reply to your brief and forbearing criticism with an even briefer modest defence.

I shall deal with only one point. If I doubt man's destiny to climb by way of civilisation to a state of greater perfection, if I see in life a continual struggle between Eros and the death instinct, the outcome of which seems to me to be indeterminable, I do not believe that in coming to those conclusions I have been influenced by innate constitutional factors or acquired emotional attitudes. I am neither a self-tormentor nor

[1] The alsatian belonging to Freud's daughter Anna

am I cussed[1] and, if I could, I should gladly do as others do and bestow upon mankind a rosy future, and I should find it much more beautiful and consoling if we could count on such a thing. But this seems to me to be yet another instance of illusion (wish fulfilment) in conflict with truth. The question is not what belief is more pleasing or more comfortable or more advantageous to life, but of what may approximate more closely to the puzzling reality that lies outside us. The death instinct is not a requirement of my heart; it seems to me to be only an inevitable assumption on .both biological and psychological grounds. The rest follows from that. Thus to me my pessimism seems a conclusion, while the optimism of my opponents seems an *a priori* assumption. I might also say that I have concluded a marriage of reason with my gloomy theories, while others live with theirs in a love-match. I hope they will gain greater happiness from this than I.

Of course it is very possible that I may be mistaken on all three points, the independence of my theories from my disposition, the validity of my arguments on their behalf, and their content. You know that the more magnificent the prospeet the lesser the certainty and the greater the passion–in which we do not wish to be involved–with which men take sides.

I can imagine that several million years ago in the Triassic age all the great -odons and -therias were very proud of the development of the Saurian race and looked forward to heaven knows what magnificent future for themselves. And then, with the exception of the wretched crocodile, they all died out. You will object that these Saurians thought nothing of the sort, that they thought of nothing but filling their bellies, while man is equipped with mind, which gives him the right to think about and believe in his future. Now, there is certainly something special about mind, so little is known about it and its relation to nature. I personally have a vast respect for mind, but has nature? Mind is only a little bit of nature, the rest of which seems to be able to get along very well

[1] Freud here uses the Viennese word *Bosnickel*

133

without it. Will it really allow itself to be influenced to any great extent by regard for mind?

Enviable he who can feel more confident about that than I.

With cordial greetings,

Yours,

Freud

PFISTER TO FREUD   *2637 Durant Avenue,*

Berkeley,

31.7.1930

. . . I am writing a lecture for the psycho-analytical society in New York on 'The Origin and Conquest of Anxiety and Obsession in Judaeo-Christian Religious History'. It is a subject which has been in my mind for years, and it first attracted my attention because it provided such magnificent corroboration of your theories. But then big new problems presented themselves, such, for instance, as the substitution of the doctrine of revenge and sacrifice by the principle of love and forgiveness. My principle of psychological continuity make it easy for me to understand the practice of sacrifice. The need for retribution has been magnificently elucidated by your work in recent years. In regard to the genuinely Christian conception of forgiveness, as represented, for instance, in the parable of the prodigal son (St Luke, xv), there is obviously a regression to the childhood state in which the child is not yet treated by the standard of good and evil, but simply with love and kindness. However, that does not solve the real problem. The application of the principle of retribution or forgiveness is among the most difficult things in education. We always have to set up rules, which leads to all sorts of trouble, until we are forced to overthrow the rules and return to the original intention. Is there not analytic action in all acts of grace and forgiveness? . . .

It always gives me great pleasure to see the great stream that bears your name growing stronger, deepening its bed, and widening.

134

My wife had a piece of news for me on her arrival that gave me great pleasure. I had carefully preserved your letters since 1909 and kept them in a box on the floor. After my first wife's death I had a house-maid who inexcusably burnt some of my most valuable papers and robbed me dreadfully. After her departure I hunted for the box in vain and gave it up for lost. Now the letters have fortunately been found. I cannot tell you how much my correspondence with you has meant to me, and how much stimulus I have derived from it. I am greatly looking forward to seeing your kind and sagacious letters again when I return to Zürich in the middle of November. . . .

Grundlsee,
20.8.1930

Dear Dr Pfister,

Just a line to let you know that I have received your letters and am following your progress in Dollaria with interest.

We are very comfortable here. My mother was ninety-five yesterday. I am amazed at how old I am myself. I am no less amazed at having been awarded the Goethe Prize of the city of Frankfurt. Our Nestroy,[1] the Vienna Aristophanes, used to say that everyone becomes a privy councillor in the end, only he doesn't always live to see it.

Cordially yours,
Freud

PFISTER TO FREUD

2637 Durant Avenue,
Berkeley,
5.9.30

. . . During the past few days I have again re-read – perhaps for the tenth time – your *The Ego and the Id*, and I felt glad that after writing it you turned to the garden of humanity, having previously, so to speak, examined the foundations and drains of its houses. One thing surprises me

[1] Johann Nepomuk Nestroy (1801–62), Austrian popular dramatist

135

greatly, but perhaps I have not fully understood you. You believe human beings to be so conservative, and talk of identification and formation of the ego-ideal through the parents. Am I wrong in rather seeing the drive to outdo the parents everywhere at work? I do not deny that the boy occasionally really identifies himself with his father, *i.e.*, wishes to be his father. He can also be said to introject his idealised father. But that gives a different look to mental life. I have the impression that conservatives all have a kink in the form of inferiority feelings, and that anyone who wants to be like his father feels himself inferior to him. Does the chief difference between man and the animals perhaps not reside in the fact that we aspire to climb higher, over the dead and the images of our parents, while the ape, in so far as he is not urged forward by the not completely conservative nature of his phylogenesis, is content to go on hanging to his father's tail? Many use the term 'identification' recklessly, and confuse it with assimilation or partial introjection.

It seems to me from your new ideas that the ego-ideal ought to be more thoroughly dealt with than it is by many. I do not attain the objective with my patients by devaluing it as a mere apeing of the parents. Just as real love does not disappear when it is made clear that the first love-object was the mother, so does the ego-ideal not collapse when it is revealed that it originated in the parents' house. The parents may be right, and their moral demands may be the correct expression of a valid order of things analogous to the hygienic order. By dethroning the ego-ideal nothing is achieved. Immoralism cannot possibly be the last word, otherwise hypocrisy and lies would be as good and valuable as honesty and integrity, and battling with drawn sword for the truth would be nothing but folly. Your morality, my dear professor, made a deep impact on me; I say this though I know that it will make you smile, because it sounds so moral, goody-goody and childish. But I am oppressed by the lack of seriousness with which some of your pupils regard confrontation with the highest ethical values and dismiss all problems with the flat phrase 'self-forgiveness', which on psychological grounds alone does not apply to deeper natures.

I prefer to deal analytically with the moral imperative, which I regard as an inadequate expression of a system of imperatives intended for the good of mankind. If this highest biological and ethical principle is deprived of its moral impulse, the effect is oppressive and alarming, while the re-establishment of the higher meaning leads to release and healing. Analysis paves the way to independence instead of a heteronomous morality. Achieving the will to moral behaviour involves sublimation, or rather the organisation of the total personality, the instincts included. In this respect sublimation, understood as a transition to non-sexual functions, does not get one very far. What I mean is that a love of mankind must lie even behind mathematics, otherwise we get the ugly picture of the calculating-machine man. I prefer complete moralisation; love of mankind always carries a strong dose of libido cathexis in the narrower sense. . . .

Berggasse 19,
Vienna IX,
12.5.1931

Dear Dr Pfister,

After another major operation I am fit for little and uncheerful but, if I have got back to some kind of synthesis again by the end of the month–that is what I have been promised–am I to miss the opportunity of seeing my old but by God's grace rejuvenated friend[1] here? Certainly not, I count on it.

Cordially yours,
Freud

---

[1] A reference to Pfister's remarriage

Dear Professor Freud,
   Your letter moved me deeply. Nothing was known here
about your operation. Only Sarasin had heard a rumour.
That you wrote so kindly in spite of your painful experience
is yet another proof of your love and a sign of the by no means
just-lived-and-taken-for-granted moral code which you always refuse to formulate. I feel tempted to base an individual
and social code of mental hygiene on you as a model.
   Meanwhile I am tremendously looking forward to seeing
you. I shall take the liberty of telephoning first. My address
in Vienna will be Congress of Religious Psychology, Vorsaal
des Kleinen Festsaal der Universität.
   You do not like people mentioning your illness. But all the
same you know how much . . .
                With cordial greetings from your grateful
                                                        Pfister

   . . . I have been greatly touched by the great sacrifices you
have made for the psycho-analytic publishing house, and
thus for the psycho-analytic movement. I cannot help again
regarding you as the noble Nathan who is so much better
than the nominal Christians. It would be a disgrace if we,
who owe so much to the publishing house, left it in the lurch,
or simply left the burdens to your strong shoulders. We have
agreed unanimously that your wishes must and shall be
carried out so far as lies in our power. . . .

PFISTER TO FREUD   *Zürich,*
                                                    24.5.33
Dear Professor Freud,

I heard the news of Ferenczi's death last night. I am deeply grieved at the loss of your distinguished champion, and I wish to share my sorrow with you. With Abraham he was the man who most thoroughly imbibed, not only your ideas, but also your spirit and, thus impelled and qualified, planted the banner of psycho-analysis in more and more new countries. In particular his brilliant discoveries about the psychology of philosophical thought, and metaphysical thought in particular, made me a grateful admirer of the modest man, and I was glad to have the opportunity during the war of forwarding his correspondence to America, though in doing so I had no suspicion that I was playing the part of a *postillon d'amour*. I hope he crossed into the land of the unconscious without pain.

The loss of this doughty champion is quite specially painful in these bedevilled, mindless times. . . .

I paid a brief visit to Germany last week, and it will be a long time before I am able to get rid of the feeling of disgust I got there. The proletarian militarism there stinks even more evilly than the blue-blooded *Junker* spirit of the Wilhelmine era. Cowardly towards the outside world, it wreaks its infantile rage on defenceless Jews, and even loots the libraries. Good luck to him who in the face of such crass idiocy still has the strength to be a doctor of souls. . . .

                                                    Hohe Warte 46,
                                                    Vienna XIX,
                                                    28.5.1933
Dear Dr Pfister,

I thank you very warmly for your letter of sympathy on Ferenczi's death. I deserve it, for the loss is very distressing. True, it was not unexpected. For the past two years our friend had not been himself; he suffered from pernicious anaemia with motor disturbances and mentally had changed very much; finally he died of asphyxia. He will remain in our memory as he was during the previous twenty years. I am of the opinion that some of his work, his genital theory, for instance, will preserve his memory for a long time.[1]

I was very pleased to hear such good news of you. Our horizon has been darkly clouded by the events in Germany. Three members of my family, two sons and a son-in-law, are looking for a new country and have not yet found one. Switzerland is not one of the hospitable countries. There has been little occasion for me to change my opinion of human nature, particularly the Christian Aryan variety. My exchange of letters with Einstein has been published simultaneously in German, French and English, but in Germany it can be neither advertised nor sold.

Martin will be coming to Zürich again soon.

With cordial greetings,

Yours,

Freud

PFISTER TO FREUD   *Zürich,*
                                                   17.2.34

. . . Reich's book on character analysis is very startling and is the subject of lively discussion. Some of it is very attractive, but some very surprising indeed. Is it not going too far to postpone all analytic interpretation until the ego resistance has been broken? Is it not wrong that the positive transference cannot be dissolved? I thought that everything false and disturbing could and had to be resolved. To me and many others it seems desirable that you should lead off the discussion of Reich's innovations in our journals and monographs. The question whether one should be so economical with interpretations seems to me to be especially important.

---

[1] *Versuch einer Genitaltheorie*, Internationaler Psychoanalytischer Verlag, Leipzig, Vienna, Zürich, 1924. (*Thalassa: a Theory of Genitality*, New York, *Psycho-Analytic Quarterly*, 1933-4)

Hitherto I have taken careful regard of the patient's digestive ability, not to the need of producing a crisis in him. Is the crisis or surprise technique really so important? Some experiences speak for it, some against. . . .

Strassergasse 47,
Vienna XIX,
13.6.1934

Dear Dr Pfister,

I congratulate you on your honorary degree, but cannot agree to your passing on to me the honour conferred on you; as the champion of religion against my *Future of an Illusion* you have the sole right to it. The fact that the Geneva theological faculty was not deterred by psycho-analysis is at least worthy of recognition.

With cordial greetings,
Yours,
Freud

PFISTER TO FREUD *Zürich,*
8.11.1934

Dear Professor Freud,

Will it not bore you if I send you another translation of my little educational book?[1] It has now appeared in German, French, English, Italian, Spanish, Polish, Greek and finally Danish. I hope that it will at least stimulate an appetite for less easily digestible fare. The introduction is by one of Denmark's leading theologians, a bishop,[2] cathedral preacher and university professor, who came to me for analysis four years ago. Unfortunately he was able to remain here for only a few weeks, but he was deeply impressed by the depth and power of analysis, as was the case incidentally with another Scandinavian bishop. I acquired a great respect for

---

[1] The Danish version of Pfister's *Psycho-analysis in the Service of Education*
[2] The Norwegian Bishop Bergrav

the intelligence and integrity of both men. Their sense of reality exceeded that of a number of prejudiced natural scientists, and they gave up their doubts only after the strongest resistance.

The Lucerne congress has certainly yielded good fruits. We are no longer in the great age when, because of your intervention, each congress gave birth to tremendous discoveries and one returned home astonished and rejoicing. No more new continents are discovered and handed over to pioneers to explore. Now the age of colonisation has set in, rich in detailed work, groping forward and searching, and also rich in errors and mistakes, reminiscent of the times of the first creative miracles of analysis and its 'Let there be light'. Unfortunately I was unable to be present at the climax of the meeting, the last day, as I was detained professionally. I am told, however, that it was the best of all. In any case the members of the various national societies grew closer to each other again, and the feeling was conveyed that the International Psycho-Analytical Association is now a strong organisation, well fortified against all sorts of shocks. . . .

Berggasse 19,
Vienna IX,
25.11.1934

Dear Dr Pfister,
Your little book which has now reached me in its new linguistic guise has had a fine career, and has certainly done good work for analysis at each of its stopping-places. I am delighted at all your successes. That you should be such a convinced analyst and at the same time a clerical gentleman is one of the contradictions that make life so interesting.

I have heard from all quarters that the Lucerne congress left behind a strong impression of firm cohesion among analysts. Perhaps the times immediately ahead will put the organisation to the test. Things are so bad everywhere in the world, why should analysis have it any easier? Of course everyone of us hopes he will be an exception and that his friends will be the same.

With cordial greetings,

Yours,

Freud

Berggasse 19,

Vienna IX,

31.1.1936

Dear Dr Pfister,

Yes, it is a piece of unexpected good news,[1] but not without its difficulties. It is not to be expected that it will go through without some legal complications. By a fortunate coincidence my son Martin will be going to Zürich in the next few days. He will call on you and discuss the whole matter. As he is a lawyer and publisher, he is in the best possible position to form an opinion. I think you should prepare a copy of the will for him immediately. Let me not omit to express my sympathy for the poor young man who faces the end of life at such an early age.

My state of health generally is good, though I am very much plagued and hampered by the local complaint in my mouth. My daughter, who has taken complete charge of looking after me, strongly objects to the congress's being held at a distant place, because she does not want to leave me. If the choice does not fall on a near place, she will probably not attend.

Special reasons for declining a *Festschrift* and all that sort of thing do not seem to me to be called for. An eightieth birthday is hardly an event that calls for celebration.

I am glad that you and your family are well.

With cordial greetings,

Yours,

Freud

[1] A young American patient of Pfister's had left a will in favour of the publishing house

Berggasse 19,
Vienna IX,
27.3.37

Dear Dr Pfister,

How delightful to hear from you again after a long interval. Can I assume that you and yours are well? I have handed over Mr G.'s letter to my son, who will deal with it. Let us wish the generous benefactor a long life, if he is able to enjoy it.

My daughter will certainly gladly accept your report; she will hardly dispute that her files are incomplete. Actually I do not deserve your reproach for not writing anything. I have finished a sizeable piece about some significant matters,[1] but because of external considerations, or rather dangers, it cannot be published. It is again about religion, so again it will not be pleasing to you. So only a few short papers have been usable for the Almanac and *Imago*.

With cordial greetings,
Yours,
Freud

PFISTER TO FREUD

Zürich,
12.3.38

Dear Professor Freud,

Shaken to the depths as I am by the events taking place in Austria, I cannot omit expressing my most profound sympathy with you and offering you all the help that lies in my power. I should be delighted if there were anything practical I could do to demonstrate the gratitude that I feel towards you. The lecture I am giving to-night again reminds me of the tremendous amount that science has to thank you for. I am convinced that every member of the Psycho-Analytical Society will be proud of the opportunity of being of service to you and your delightful family.

In cordial gratitude and friendship,
Yours,
Pfister

---

[1] *Moses and Monotheism*, Standard Ed. Vol. XXIII

Berghaldenstrasse 34,
Zürich VII,
12.12.1939

Last Saturday the Swiss Psycho-Analytic Society held a memorial meeting in honour of your great husband in the cantonal mental hospital of Königsfelden, canton of Aargau. Our president, Dr Sarasin, in a warm and deeply felt speech presented us with a character portrait of the brilliant and yet so infinitely kindly Titan. It was left to me to read to the assembly extracts from the 134 letters from the brilliant scientist and paternal friend that I have preserved. I also described to them conversations and meetings with him extending over about thirty years. After me Dr Meng spoke about the significance of Sigmund Freud. The occasion was not for the purpose of doing homage to the dead man to whom we have such a tremendous amount to be grateful for, but a profession of loyalty to the living Freud, to whom we can pay off a small part of our debt of gratitude, not by expressing our admiration and veneration, but only by cultivating his work.

In examining your husband's letters it was with both grief and pleasure that I was once again reminded of how infinitely much his family meant to him. I vividly remember his introducing me to you, his three fine sons, the vital Sophie, and the little mother of the lizards on April 25, 1909. I, who grew up fatherless and suffered for a life-time under a soft, one-sided bringing up, was dazzled by the beauty of that family life, which in spite of the almost superhuman greatness of the father of the house and his deep seriousness, breathed freedom and cheerfulness, thanks to his love and sparkling humour. In your house one felt as in a sunny spring garden, heard the gay song of larks and blackbirds, saw bright flower-beds, and had a premonition of the rich blessing of summer. To the visitor it was immediately evident that a large part of that blessing was to be attributed to you, and that you, with your gentle, kindly nature, kept putting fresh weapons into your husband's hands in the fierce battle of life. The more human beings struck him as trash (he used that expression once in his letters), the more the 'grim divine pair Ananke and Logos' (that is his own phrase too) forced him into their grim service, the more need he had of you, and without you even the giant that he was would have been unable to achieve the tremendous task on behalf of good-for-nothing humanity that his life-work represents. His letters show that his friends also meant much to him, and the fact that I had the privilege of counting among his closest friends cheered me in the sad business of paying him tribute.

Now and in later years it must be a satisfaction to you and your children to remember how much you contributed to mitigating your husband's internal and also external sufferings and the tragedy of his old age by your goodness and piety. From the letter of your daughter Anna to our president we learnt with pleasure how capable of enjoyment the great tolerator remained to the end. For that he was indebted to all of you. On September 21, 1926, your husband wrote to me saying how glad he was that his daughter was beginning to do good work in the field of psycho-analytic pedagogics, which I inaugurated and was the only application of psychoanalysis which was flourishing.

During the last few years I have often thought of a striking passage in his letter of June 3, 1910, which I believe I should now quote to you. It was as follows:

I cannot face with comfort the idea of life without work; work and the free play of the imagination are for me the same thing, I take no pleasure in anything else. That would be a recipe for happiness but for the appalling thought that productivity is entirely dependent on a sensitive disposition. What would one do when ideas failed or words refused to come? It is impossible not to shudder at the thought. Hence, in spite of all the acceptance of fate which is appropriate to an honest man, I have one quite secret prayer: that I may be spared any wasting away and crippling of my ability to work because of physical deterioration. In the words of King Macbeth, let us die in harness.

146

At any rate his wish for mental rest after dying in the royal harness of the thinker has now been fulfilled.

Your husband's letters are among my most cherished possessions. As long as I live I shall always have them by my side. With my sixty-seven years I have myself now reached old age and have moved into a wonderfully situated place of retirement. Mentally I still feel pretty fresh, only sometimes, though rarely, there are periods of fatigue, as on my last trip to Vienna, when my memory failed. I am working on a number of projects in which, with my feeble powers, I continue your husband's method of work. Though the unfavourable times are more willing to strike up a dance for the devil of lies than to listen to symphonies of truth, I believe with your husband: *La vérité est en marche.*

With cordial greetings to you and your children, and especially Fräulein Anna and Dr Martin.

With deep devotion,

Yours,

Pfister

Frau Professor Dr Freud,
20 Maresfield Gardens,
London, N.W.3

INDEX

149

www.ingramcontent.com/pod-product-compliance
Lightning Source LLC
Chambersburg PA
CBHW050842270326
41930CB00019B/3439